FORGETTING
OURSELVES
ON PURPOSE

FORGETTING
OURSELVES
ON PURPOSE

VOCATION
AND THE
ETHICS OF
AMBITION

BRIAN J. MAHAN
Foreword by Robert Coles

JOSSEY-BASS
A Wiley Company
www.josseybass.com

Published by

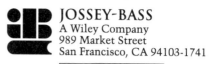

JOSSEY-BASS
A Wiley Company
989 Market Street
San Francisco, CA 94103-1741

www.josseybass.com

Jossey-Bass books and products are available through most bookstores.
To contact Jossey-Bass directly, call (888) 378-2537, fax to (800) 605-2665,
or visit our Web site at www.josseybass.com.

Substantial discounts on bulk quantities of Jossey-Bass books are available to
corporations, professional associations, and other organizations. For details
and discount information, contact the special sales department at Jossey-Bass.

We at Jossey-Bass strive to use the most environmentally sensitive paper stocks available
to us. Our publications are printed on acid-free recycled stock whenever possible, and
our paper always meets or exceeds minimum GPO and EPA requirements.

Library of Congress Cataloging-in-Publication Data

Mahan, Brian.
Forgetting ourselves on purpose: vocation and the ethics of
ambition / Brian J. Mahan; foreword by Robert Coles.—1st ed.
p. cm.
Includes bibliographical references and index.
ISBN 0-7879-5633-3 (alk. paper)
1. Ambition. I. Title.
BJ1533.A4 M24 2002
179'.9—dc21   2001004897

FIRST EDITION
HB Printing   10 9 8 7 6 5 4 3 2 1

CONTENTS

CONTENTS

Hi, Ma!

Foreword

In the pages ahead an American teacher and philosopher looks resolutely inward at himself and attentively, thoughtfully, outward at so many of us who are trying to get along as best we can in early-twenty-first-century America. Here, then, is moral and psychological introspection put in the service of social and cultural circumspection in the earnest hope that we who want to further ourselves—to get ahead and become successful—will not, in so doing, become lost to ourselves and, not least, to all those others with whom we live and work. This is no small task for a writer to attempt—that his ethical concerns become conveyed to readers in such a way that we take serious notice, yet do not feel patronized or even scolded or condemned. Critics, of course, have every right to distance themselves from what (and those whom) they find objectionable, but those who would persuade, as well as promulgate decisively, had best keep in mind their own links to perceived threats of error, of wrong-doing. Such a warning need not be directed at this book's author. Drawing on the book's jacket—the suggestive picture it offers: a climb up a ladder is fraught with danger (one can fall on one's face), and so we ought to take our steps with a certain caution—a kind of awareness, Mahan reminds us, that will inform our body's moves, even as our eyes (and our mind's striving impulses) pay due and necessary respect to what it is, up there, that we seek, and why, lest otherwise, we climb so hurriedly, lustily, that we misstep (morally as well as literally) and take a fall that hurts us with bruises of shame, confusion, despair (a sense that we've got a lot, with more to come, and yet seem purposely astray, if not awry).

This extraordinarily warm-hearted and kindly book reaches out to us with the knowing and telling reassurance that moral inwardness can prompt us, if we are willing, to link arms with others rather than hold them off as distant (and alas, reproved) others. Yes, the subject matter ahead reminds us that we all too commonly "forget ourselves"—lose track of life's big moral whys and whithers. But many of us who read books and wonder to ourselves and with others about our reasons, our purposes, are also intent on figuring things out, not only in the hope of getting someplace, but with the wish for self-respect upon arrival, and a modicum of money (and the attendant approval) that goes along with such an accomplished errand.

No wonder, then, that some of us, heeding Brian Mahan's summons to self-consultation, even self-communing, will take note of the Augustinian side of his mind's life: his response to the morally awake American psychologist, William James, and the morally awake American novelist, Walker Percy—two physicians who took note of the soulful yearning for moral direction in many who at times seem wholly committed to the empirical materialism that gets regarded as ordinary business in our contemporary secular world. James tried to understand our willfulness, but he knew that the exertion of the self has to be examined morally as well as instrumentally (how, and to what end, an effort is affirmed as well as how effectively it gets put into action). So with Dr. Percy—he smirked wryly, sometimes sadly, at himself and others: the throng of us, going through our days and ways, all too oblivious with respect to our intentions and aspirations as members of various communities, as well as individuals bent on this or that solo stunt. In his own brief way, amidst a discussion of his writing life, Dr. Percy was asserting what Professor Mahan wants us to hear in our minds as we move across time in this one and only chance we have as human beings, here on this planet—the importance of getting it right as we proceed to get our jobs, our earthly satisfactions, achievements.

I suppose the irony that Dr. Percy mobilizes in his story-telling is the same irony this wonderfully lucid, and clear-headed and compelling book addresses—that we who want to soar (and why not!) also need to take stock of ourselves, lest a possible anguish of heart, mind, soul, befalls us. "We seek moral companions," Dr. Percy once remarked—and then a melancholy reservation: "The problem is, we sometimes don't know that, and so don't find what we really yearn to find." For sure, I gratefully feel that the fine deed Brian Mahan has wrought in accomplishing this book will offer that moral companionship to so many of us readers—lucky, indeed, to have the pages ahead as a presence in our eagerly inquiring, searching lives.

August 2001   ROBERT COLES

Preface—And an Invitation

WHAT THIS BOOK IS ABOUT

Forgetting Ourselves on Purpose grows out of a course I taught to undergraduates at the University of Colorado for nearly a decade. More recently, over the last five years to be exact, I have taught "The Ethics of Ambition" both to seminary students at Emory University's Candler School of Theology and to rising high school seniors who have made their way to Atlanta to attend the Youth Theology Institute, also housed on the Emory campus. I have taught it as a seminar and as a large lecture course, recast it for workshops and retreats, and abridged it for an evening adult education program.

The course was popular from the start. The reasons for its popularity remain something of a mystery, though I think people's reaction to the word *ambition* has something to do with it. When I would ask my students at Colorado whether ambition is a desirable character trait, the overwhelming response was, "Well, of course it is." Few expressed reservations of any kind. Many seemed surprised that I'd even ask.

Colleagues of my own vintage are more cautious about ambition. They often assume from the course's title that it intends to deconstruct the prevalent images of success in American society. It occurred to me that many of my colleagues were undergraduates in the sixties, as I was, and that their suspicions regarding ambition represent something of an aberration, an opinion out of line with both earlier and later generations. Over the last five or six years, however, I have discovered that seminarians and high school theologians, as well as adult church groups, also tend to be less than sanguine about ambition.

If you look up *ambition* in the *Oxford English Dictionary*, you'll find little enthusiasm for it there. Shakespeare's admonition, "by that sin fell the angels," is quoted, as is another author's opinion that ambition is a "puffed-up greedy humor." As for its derivation, *ambition* comes from the Latin *ambitio*, which in its original context refers to politicians ambling around Rome trying to solicit votes. Even *Webster's* more recent definition of ambition as "an ardent desire for rank, fame, or power" has a bad feel to it.[1]

So why such discordant voices about a seemingly straightforward term like *ambition*? Why the tension between the generations, or between undergraduates and divinity students? I can't tell you exactly, but when a term provokes mutually exclusive pronouncements delivered with roughly equivalent degrees of self-assurance, there's something there worth investigating.

The practices, reflections, and arguments contained in this book build on the insights, observations, and opinions that have emerged from my teaching over nearly two decades. It is the product of many midcourse corrections and of incessant tinkering and recalibration.

The practices and commentary you find in this book do not demand mastery of a particular body of knowledge or passive submission to a particular line of argumentation. What you find here, then, is an open-ended approach to things, one that leaves room for careful and extended scrutiny of the idiosyncratic preoccupations that you bring to this book.[2]

Specifically, I encourage you to engage with the inevitable tension between the self perceived as morally responsible or spiritually advanced and the self perceived as successful in the more banal, everyday sense of the word. It calls attention to the all-too-human tendency to deny knowledge of the incompatibility between these two self-perceptions, either by repressing so-called worldly ambition in order to cultivate and protect an image of the self as moral or by the equally suspect stratagem of giving up on the moral enterprise altogether in the hope of competing efficaciously in the marketplace of worldly success.

Of course, we'd like to believe that our ambition only rarely conflicts with our nobler aspirations, both moral and spiritual, and that we rarely have to choose between them. We would like to believe that our personal triumphs somehow trickle down and enrich the rest of humanity and that when we pursue what we judge best for ourselves, the rest of the universe conveniently falls into place.

But we know better. William James tells us that he would like to be both a saint and a millionaire but admits that what he does to achieve the latter would probably disqualify him from the former. James does not mean to suggest by this that it is a bad thing to be a millionaire, or even that it is better to be a saint. Perhaps he wishes only to avoid deluding himself into believing that the best way to become a saint is to be a millionaire.[3]

But I'm getting ahead of myself. Not only that, but I'm beginning to sound a little moralistic, which is exactly what I'd like to avoid. In fact, I am convinced, though it may well take most of this book to make my case, that whether we know it or not—or, better, whether we remember it or not—what we'd most like to do is chuck the whole project of improving ourselves and with it our incessant and obsessive monitoring of our "progress" toward whoever it is we think we ought to be. That is to say, we long for a kind of self-forgetful yet fully engaged sense of immediacy, for a more graced and gracious way of being in this world, one that cuts deeper than the surface imagery sketched by our infernal preoccupation with some soon-to-be success or failure (financial, social, or spiritual).

For starters, then, let me simply present you with an invitation to a life increasingly given over to self-forgetfulness, to the delightfully nonmoral discipline of remembering to forget ourselves on purpose. The words are Thomas Merton's, though the invitation is from God: "The more we persist in misunderstanding the phenomena of life, the more we analyze them out into strange finalities and complex purposes of our own, the more we involve ourselves in sadness, absurdity and despair. . . . Yet the fact remains that we are invited to forget ourselves on purpose, cast our awful solemnity to the winds and join in the general dance."[4]

WHAT THIS BOOK DOES

Several years ago, my spiritual director, a Catholic nun who plays the harp and says that I'm uncomfortable with my body, ordered me to attend a sacred dance workshop.[5] Once there, I provoked anger in a wide variety of holy people. I accomplished this sometimes by sprinting off in the wrong direction, sometimes by making a full spin instead of a half spin. But most of the time, I just failed to distinguish my left foot from my right foot in time.

"No, Brian, the other left," that sacred chorus intoned solemnly, echoing earlier tormentors still reverberating in my kinesthetic superego.

No doubt about it, Merton's passed-along invitation to join in the general dance inspires; but it also intimidates. It's compelling enough, but it's menacing too. I wonder if anything is more likely to intensify self-consciousness to an unbearable level than an invitation to "forget ourselves on purpose."

The trouble here is twofold. In the first place, the notion of watching ourselves getting better at forgetting ourselves is absurd on the face of it. It is also self-hateful. It assumes that, if we are to become more spiritual, more compassionate, more centered, more whatever it is we want to become, we must disdain the self available to us now. This assumption is so widespread, so insistently reinforced by various social sanctions and rewards, that any attempt to challenge it is either greeted with incredulity or dismissed as unduly pessimistic.

But there is paradox here: if we can't chase after self-forgetfulness, how are we ever going to catch up with it? Merton, to his credit, does not answer this question directly. He does however, proffer a couple of questions easily reframed to address our present situation: "If you want to identify me, ask me not where I live, or what I like to eat, or how I comb my hair, but ask me what I think I am living for, in detail, and ask me what I think is keeping me from living fully for the thing I want to live for."[6]

Good questions, and telling ones too. In fact, the two practices that give structure, direction, and texture to this book—"formative remembering" and "spiritual indirection"—pose, after their own fashion, these very questions over and over again and in varying contexts.

HOW TO READ THIS BOOK

Reading this book is not a spectator sport. It requires active engagement. I do not try to argue you into insight. Arguments tend to move in straight lines toward thin resolutions. We'll be moving in circles instead, and each time around we're likely to cut a little more deeply into the subsoil of our own experience.

Returning to the dance metaphor, let me say that this book wishes to avoid becoming the spiritual equivalent of an Arthur Murray dance studio. I do not ask you to place your feet into a series of painted steps in rapid succession and then call it dancing. That may be what you'd like me to do, but frankly, I'd rather forsake the appearance of being helpful if it means setting you up for a fall.

You know it as well as I do: we learn to dance by dancing. "But something is bound to go wrong," you might be thinking. Yes, something *will* go wrong—more than one thing, most likely. That's where the learning happens. The point here is not so much to get better, but to gently coax ourselves away from "I'm terrified I'll step on somebody's feet" and toward "You'll never guess who I bumped into today." The rest takes care of itself.

One more thing before we get under way. Were I to describe this book and the practices and reflections contained within it in a single phrase, I'd describe it as a prolonged mnemonic device, a kind of educational aid for remembering what you already know but have been strong-armed into forgetting. So let me issue an invitation of my own—an invitation to remember that the dance music is always and already playing wherever you are, wherever you've been, wherever you're headed. If you listen attentively enough, I think you're likely to remember something else: you've been dancing to it all along. You're dancing to it now.

Shall we?

August 2001   BRIAN J. MAHAN
Atlanta, Georgia

Acknowledgments

The Boulder Crew: I wish to express special appreciation to Jack Kelso, former Director of the Farrand Residential Academic Program at the University of Colorado at Boulder, with whom I first hashed out the ideas for the course that ultimately gave birth to this book, and to Cathy Comstock and Jim Palmer, also of the Farrand Residential Academic Program, for their support of my teaching at Farrand and for many valuable conversations on the subject matter treated here.

Special thanks to Mike and Pam Smith for their friendship and encouragement, and to Bruce Ronda and Mike Hirota for helping out from start to finish.

I would also like to thank the following friends, colleagues, and former students: Marilyn Krysl, LeRoy Moore, Elise Boulding, Lynnette Westerlund, Marie Wilwerding Venner, Brad Venner, Wynne Maggi, Steve Byers, Gregg Goldstein, Priscilla Inkpen, Sr. Rose Liddell, Sr. Cecelia Linnenbrink, Nick Helburn, J. McKim Malville, and many others who I hope will forgive their omission here.

The Atlanta Crew: I owe a special debt to my friend Jim Fowler who read and commented on each chapter as it appeared and who helped me think things through from start to finish. The case study of John Dean in his *Stages of Faith* first got me thinking about the issues addressed in this book.

I would also like to express appreciation to Tom Frank, Steve Kraftchick, Stacia Brown, and David White for their especially careful readings of the text and to Fred Helenius for research assistance.

Other friends, colleagues, and former students I wish to thank are Tryggvi Arnason, Beth Corrie, Pinapue T. K. Early, Barbara Elwell, Jim Farwell, Phyllis Faust, Chuck Foster, David Graybeal, Tami Groves, J. Drew Johnson, Maggie Kulyk, Sheila McCarthy, J. Chris McKee, Hank Nelson, Lisa Persons, Ellen Purdum, Brenda Stevenson, Liberty Stewart, Tim Van Meter, Jennifer Walker, and M. Boyd Waller.

Thanks to the whole crew at Jossey-Bass, especially to Sheryl Fullerton for her editing savvy and for guiding me through the process of publishing a first book. I also wish to express my special gratitude to the late Sarah Polster of Jossey-Bass who accepted my manuscript and gave it her blessing. Thanks to Anthony Glavin for advice and encouragement and to Robert Coles, Gerald May, and Nuala O'Faolain for their encouragement.

Finally, I wish to thank my wife Kim Boykin for her editing, advice, and support throughout this process and for carrying me over the finish line.

FORGETTING
OURSELVES
ON PURPOSE

CHAPTER ONE

Ask Me What I'm Living For

DOUBTING PAM

I was in my second year of teaching at CU-Boulder when I met Pam at a Farrand Hall Christmas party. She was a senior.

"So, Pam," I asked, "what's up for next year?"

Pam looked as if she'd heard the question before. I've since learned not to ask seniors that kind of thing. All you're likely to get is a deep sigh and a belabored listing of two or three possibilities, delivered with the strained enthusiasm of a politician's handshake. These days, I usually make a point of saying something more like, "Oh, so you're a senior. You'll probably be doing a lot of traveling next year while you decide what to do next." I get a much better reaction that way. But Pam was polite.

"Well, it looks like I'll be going into the Peace Corps," she told me.

"You will?! Wonderful. Was it a difficult decision for you? I mean, had you thought about grad school at all, or anything?"

"Yeah, actually, it was a difficult decision, a very difficult one, really . . . because I was accepted at Yale Law School too."

"I can certainly see why that would be difficult. I mean, yeah, Yale Law School."

I don't remember the rest of what we talked about, but the Yale-Peace Corps dilemma is inscribed forever in my memory, and with good reason.

It was the very next day in class that my mind went blank in the middle of a lecture. That kind of thing happened to me in my first couple of years of teaching. My face pulsed like an artery. I was completely lost. It was all I could do not to run out of the room screaming, head in hands. Then, thank God, my conversation with Pam came to mind.

"By the way," I said nonchalantly, emerging from my panicky blankness, "I meant to mention something to you earlier. Yesterday at the Farrand Christmas—I mean, holiday—party (I saw a couple of you there), I met a young woman, Pam. Maybe some of you know her. Anyway, Pam's going into the Peace Corps even though she was accepted by Yale Law School. You know, she was a little distressed by her dilemma, but she sounded pretty sure about her choice as far as I could tell. So, what do you think about that? What would you have done? Anybody?"

This throwaway question, intended to do little more than jump start my neurons, generated a conversation that lasted for two class periods and moved through three distinct phases. In the first phase of the conversation, Pam's decision was thought to be self-validating and unworthy of further comment, a reaction conforming almost perfectly to a familiar style of laissez-faire individualism that I have come to expect in this kind of situation.

"Well, if that's what she wants . . . you know . . . why not? Who's to say what's the best thing for somebody else?"

"Well, I'd probably have gone to Yale. I'd like that. But it's fine that Pam chose the Peace Corps. More power to her."

"Right, well, I have this friend who spent a year in Belize in the Peace Corps also. And he thought that he got more out of being with them than he gave them. It was really rewarding. So, I can see it. I'm not sure why you're even asking, though."

"Hmm. I guess she just likes helping other people more than making money. And so, what's the deal? We could use more people like Pam, I think."

The second phase of the conversation took a more self-reflective and critical turn. The initial consensus—that there was really no reason to be examining Pam's motives in the first place—slowly gave way to several questions of the I-was-just-wondering type.

"Hmm. Do you remember . . . ah . . . well, did she say whether or not she applied for deferred admissions or anything? She might have. I think you can do that in law school."

"Do you think her parents were upset? They could have been really upset. You know, all that money they spent, and she had probably told them that she was going to go to law school. Then she got into Yale and didn't go. I dunno."

"Just wondering out loud here . . . Didn't she know that she could've done more for the poor if she went to Yale Law School first? If she didn't know, I think, well, she should've known, really."

The third and final stage of the conversation emerged when the gentle probing of the second phase gave way to a distinctly more aggressive and accusatory spirit.

"Well, yes," I asked, "does anybody think she might have been afraid to go to Yale? I've heard it's very competitive and really tough there. People would have been at least as bright as she was."

"Yeah, to follow up on that," came a reply, "look at it this way. She has her letter of acceptance, so she can show people she got it. She could frame it or whatever and still have that feeling of prestige and all that. Yale and everything. And she looks sensitive, too, going into the Peace Corps. So, I guess the question here is, what's she trying to prove? You know what I mean? I mean, what's she trying to prove?"

Despite the escalating rhetoric of this third stage of the conversation, many of us were caught off guard by the statement of a young man who seemed self-conscious about revealing what he had on his mind.

"I don't mean to be insensitive, but did it occur to you that, well, she might have lied to you—that maybe she didn't really get into Yale Law School? If she got in— let's face it—I really think she would've gone."

There was a stunned silence and then a series of reluctant confessions. As it turned out, the possibility of Pam's having lied had occurred to a number of students, who had been reluctant to say so out loud. Others said that the thought was in the back of their mind somewhere, though they hadn't put it into words. Still others, especially those whose opinions held sway in the first stage of the conversation, were scandalized at the suggestion and reiterated their initial statements about leaving Pam alone to do what she had decided to do. "Why are we talking about her anyway? It's her life, right?" But no response could contradict the prolonged and restless silence we had endured together.

From that moment on, Pam's story took on a koan-like status. Poor Pam had spoken only a sentence or two, but we went on and on, ultimately speaking volumes about these few words: our capacity for imputing motives and analyzing character traits with nothing much to go on was stupefying. We just couldn't stop ourselves.

Of course, now each new class hears the story of Pam and is briefed about the three stages of that initial conversation. Now you've heard about it too. Things are getting more complicated these days. Radical new Pamological interpretations render the initial conversation naïve by comparison. It is only a matter of time until some French postcontemporary thinker chimes in with something very new and pleasingly opaque.

My own take on "the case of Pam" has evolved as well. Initially, I tended to interpret the conversation as progressively more disclosive of how deeply the class members and I had assimilated our culture's scripted expectations for success and failure. In this case, the script reads: "Choose Yale; gracefully forgo the Peace Corps." What else could explain these suspicions about Pam's straightforward decision? Unpleasant as it was, those of us burdened by such suspicions would have to admit to our more-or-less-habitual expectation that this type of script and many others like it pretty much runs the show and that apparent departures from them were the product of eccentricity or weakness—or, as in the case of Pam, of a lie.

The progression and direction of the conversation were painfully clear: the polite veneer of nonjudgmental acceptance of the first phase cracked here and there during the second, and it was unceremoniously peeled away in the third and after, revealing the hard truths none of us wished to face. Only then did we come to know and reluctantly confess what we *really* thought about Pam and her silly decision all along.

Tough-minded analysis, all right; but it was all a bit too cozy. Why is it, I wondered, that tough-minded analysis so often seems to work hand in glove with the most banal and transparent manifestations of self-interest and with uncritical embrace of what for all the world appear to be the most radically truncated images of human possibility?

I began to think back on the conversation and its interpreters with a different kind of suspicion: one regarding the sources and nature of our own suspicions regarding Pam. Might it not make more sense to see the second phase of the Pam conversation—in which her decision to forgo Yale for the Peace Corps was probed with clear self-referential intent—as more fully engaged and authentic than either the first or third phase? Think about it. The "Hey, it's her life; why are we talking about

Pam?" tone of the first phase of the conversation conveniently and politely diverted questions concerning the implications of Pam's decision for the rest of us ("Good luck, Pam. Be sure to write."). Though the argument of the third phase conflicts mightily with the first, the end product is pretty similar. If Pam is a liar, or is naïve and misguided, why bother with her? The fact that the conversation polarized between the avoidance strategy of phase one and the avoidance strategy of phase three effectively precluded return to the self-reflective questioning of phase two.

What's more, those who held firmly to the laissez-faire spirit of phase one received moral credit for "openness," while the deconstructionist Pamologists of phase three took pleasure in having once again avoided being duped by another marginally convincing, but ultimately spurious, pantomime of virtue. The lead participants of phase two—most of whom wound up adherents of openness or suspicion anyway—had no particular way of visualizing or congratulating themselves; they were too involved in the conversation. Maybe it was a setup. I certainly went for it. No one wants to be naïve, even if it means calling Pam a liar, even if it means blowing her off with a compliment, even if it means doing both simultaneously and calling it a lively conversation.

VOCATION AND AMBITION

But is resistance naïve? If not, what is the alternative to the internalized script that tells us that if you get accepted to Yale Law School then you go to Yale Law School?

When I first introduce the notion of vocation as a counterplayer to ambition, some people get confused. They are willing to admit that ambition for power or fame or wealth is the kind of thing that can get a person into trouble. Jailed stockbrokers, drugged-out rock stars, and defrocked televangelists are common illustrations.

But can learning a useful skill really be the appropriate response to the problems associated with inordinate ambition? I found this kind of response unsettling at first. It took a while to figure out that the term *vocation* connotes to some the worlds of auto repair, heavy machinery, and elementary computer programming, all manner of things you do if you can't get into college. That is, more exactly, it connotes the world of skills taught in the evening at the local high school after you've spent your day doing something even less interesting. Fortunately, the connotation is not so deeply fixed that it cannot be challenged and dislodged. This is a good thing because I think the idea of vocation is worth liberating from night school.

There are many reasons for choosing vocation as the noble and all-encompassing counterplayer to mere ambition. Some are less compelling than others. It is, for example, better to be "called" to do something than to merely decide to do it on one's own. This is evident enough to anyone who reads alumni notes. Alums invariably write in the passive voice if they wish to impress their fellow alums. Though they may wheedle, cajole, fawn, grouse, or sometimes work their way into some desired position, alums are always being "named" to this or that, or are graciously "accepting" something wonderful proffered by authoritative others who have recently detected their worthiness. They are "called."

There is another, albeit closely related, quality associated with vocation that I find considerably more enticing than anything that can be passively granted— more enticing, I suspect, than even our own most energetically repressed "worldly" ambitions. Vocation speaks of a life that is "unscripted" in a sense. By contrast, ambition seems scripted by its very essence ("If you get accepted to Yale Law School, then you go to Yale Law School"). In ambition, the prestige of the achievement often seems to depend more on the dignity of the role itself than on the dignity of the one who fills it.

This is not the case with vocation. Vocation speaks of a gracious discovery of a kind of interior consonance between our deepest desires and hopes and our unique gifts, as they are summoned forth by the needs of others and realized in response to that summons. That's what's so enticing about the idea of vocation: in embracing one's vocation, the draining internal opposition between compassion and personal ambition is, at least in principle, overcome. As Frederick Buechner says, "The place God calls you to is the place where your deep gladness and the world's deep hunger meet."[1]

The only problem is that many of us don't see things this way and would rather not take somebody else's word for it. " 'God's call'? Oh, sure, round up 'the usual suspects'—Gandhi, Mother Teresa, and Martin Luther King Jr. Yes, they lived lives like that. And we really all love them. They even make us cry sometimes. But after all, there's only three of them and, who knows, they may have done it to get into heaven or something anyway."

Once the term *vocation* is liberated from night school, it is almost immediately interpreted as standing in stark opposition to achieving success in any profession. This makes me feel uneasy, not only because I intend no such thing but also because I don't enjoy being an inverse caricature of everyday social expectations, with inversely definitive plans for everyone else's life. Vocation, it somehow comes across, has nothing to do with lawyers, doctors, investment bankers; it has to do with giving those things up. Images of the archetypal starving artist, of "my cousin's friend who teaches in Newark," of "that guy I met this summer who is a forest ranger and is really into the environment," populate our collective consciousness.

But there is more to this than meets the eye. When you come right down to it, who really likes the idea of living a scripted life? Most of us at one time or another have found ourselves pitted against some manner of insidious conformist pressure, willing perhaps at least for a time to resist whatever blandishments and sanctions an ad hoc committee that fashions social expectations might tempt or threaten us with. Not only this, but there are few of us who don't now and again yearn for a different kind of life and wonder what we should do about it.

Again, why the resistance to Pam, to the concept of vocation, to the possibility of embracing a different kind of life? I would like to be indefinite and evasive in my response to this question, in keeping with the social expectations of my own profession. But my experience demands otherwise. Let me be blunt: there is something approaching a consensus these days, at least in some quarters, that human motivation is self-interested without remainder. By *consensus*, I don't mean to suggest something consciously accepted, even less something recommended as ideal. I speak rather of something "in the air": a collective assumption of sorts.

Some, it is true, get really excited about the gospel of self-interest. Brandishing Ayn Rand's *Fountainhead* or some sociobiological or free-market facsimile, they wish to awaken the uninitiated to the virtues of egoism. Others—many others—adopt a kind of soft-edged laissez-faire approach to things. They do not try to clue you in or talk you out of anything. If spending your life working with the homeless is the kind of thing that makes you happy, that's great ("Give me a call, I'll go down to the shelter with you sometime"). Finally, others confront the presumption of ubiquitous self-interest head-on, but do so with a ferocity that serves only to underscore their own uncertainty ("Maybe you're selfish. Did you ever think you might just be selfish?").

Given all that, life conceived as vocation—life increasingly given over to compassion for self, others, and world—appears in such circumstances as benighted, beside the point, a bad bet. Still, I have often noticed a kind of wistfulness when the subject turns to the usual suspects. We doubt their relevance to our own lives, though we would rather not. We are inspired but don't know what to do about it. Often precociously fatigued and discouraged by our own suspicions, we seem nonetheless unable to shake them. Still, the usual suspects and their understudies in the artist's loft, or in Newark, or in the forest preserve seem to remind us of something we already know. It is as if we carry within us a "shadow government" of compassion and idealism.

In fact, I've come to believe that most of us wish nothing more than to liberate our shadow government from exile and to incarnate in the routines of work and play and worship the deepest longings of our heart. But the inhibitions that hold us and our longings in captivity are many and strong. We need to be better acquainted with them. We need to flush them out of their hiding place, study them in detail, and show them for what they really are.

COMPASSION IN EXILE: DICKEY'S STORY

Anyone who has ever taught a large lecture class or done much public speaking knows that people often mistake you for a television. Those who read newspapers while you're on, bring snacks, and jabber incessantly to an increasingly uncomfortable neighbor are only the tip of the iceberg, the obvious cases. Many others share with them a magical belief that although they are able to see you clearly and in detail, you cannot see them at all. Sometimes I wish that I could turn the tables on my audience and watch them that way. It's not that I'm vengeful; it's because I'd like to learn more about them. Were they televisions, the first thing I would do is switch over to VCR and hit rewind. Then I could be on the lookout for what makes so many of them dubious about Pam, about the usual suspects, and about the notion of vocation itself.

My wish was eventually granted in the way that all such wishes are granted: in a manner of speaking. I stumbled across a chapter in Robert Coles's book *Privileged Ones*, titled "A Boy's Journey from Liberalism to Social Darwinism."[2] It is the story of a young man named Dickey who lived in a wealthy suburb outside of Boston. In Coles's case study, there is something reminiscent of a war correspondent's account of the battlefield. Here was the harrowing story of a shadow government in retreat, the story of ideals marginalized and exiled, the story of youthful compassion and idealism under assault.

The children interviewed in Coles's book are junior members of America's ruling class. Coles does not say this; he does not need to. These are not multicar families, but *multihome* families. The early education of these children includes instruction on how to get along with servants, and many of Coles's subjects are seasoned world travelers by the age of ten. Dickey inhabits such a world, though he and his family are at the low end of things, comparatively speaking. They are not to the manor born, and their liberal social views are not shared by their neighbors.

In this case study, Dickey's "friendly adversary," another Richard, often chides Dickey for holding to his family's progressive ethos. There are elements of playfulness in their sparring matches, and in another time and place things might have been different. But both Richards and their families are suburban Bostonians, and it is the 1970s. Bussing is on everyone's mind, and the suburbs are being challenged to do their part. Emotions are running high, and opinion on both sides has little give. It is a time when no one in Dickey's town can avoid reflecting on matters of race and privilege. The conversation has been joined and the lines of battle drawn.

As a nine-year-old, Dickey spoke his mind, freely, persuasively, and often. He was for bussing. He was in favor of it in Boston; he was in favor of it in the public schools of his home town; and what's more, he was in favor of it in his own exclusive private school. Of course, Dickey's opinions rankled many of his classmates and no doubt raised a few eyebrows at home among parents: "Dickey had this to say: 'I think it would be a very good idea if we had some *color* around here.'"[3]

There's no need to romanticize Dickey. He was a child who thought the way his parents did. They were liberals, after all, and Dickey saw no reason to question their commitment. The strength of Dickey's allegiance to his parents and their liberalism is another matter. For a time, at least, Dickey stood by them when things got tough. He winced when Richard told him that if his parents were so hot on bussing, maybe they should pay for it themselves; but he held his ground. What's more, Dickey was not merely parroting his parents' take on things. There was an emotional intensity about his advocacy of his parents' liberal views. He was moved to compassion by what he heard and saw around him, and he wanted to do something about it. In assigned essays, he warned the black children from Boston that they might not wish to come out this way. He heard what his classmates were saying, and he knew how he would feel if their words were directed at him. Already marginalized, he did his best to stand with those who were truly excluded.

Over time, Coles's interviews reveal the cost of this protracted conflict on Dickey. Richard's unremitting challenges took their toll. His taunts stung; his words were like the point of the nail hammered home by the whole town. But it was something else that turned the tide against Dickey's attempts to hold his own and to speak from his heart. He discovered that his parents were not quite as serious about things as he was. Turning to them in a moment of disillusionment, he asked if it was possible for them to move into the city; "I'm not learning how to get along with anyone but kids like Richard." When his father told him that they were staying right where they were and that they were doing it for his own good, something gave.

It was not long before Dickey informed his parents that though he still shared their opinions about bussing and the rest, he was going to keep a low profile for a while. It was just too hard to swim against the tide. Predictably enough, Dickey's short-term strategy was really a new beginning, a radical break. By the age of thirteen, he was fully at home with his surroundings. He no longer wished to move to Boston or anywhere else. He and Richard were closer now, and he was finally invited to one of Richard's birthday parties. What's more, Dickey had a new take on things. His opinions on bussing, race, and social change had become more "realistic," more scientific. He explained it all to his parents and upset them considerably. His friends were more receptive. Blacks, it turned out, really were "different" and not quite ready to receive what they demanded, at least not now. He meant nothing harmful by this, of course. It's just the way things are. Why not admit it: "I used to think we should try to change a lot of things right away. But you shouldn't be too quick. . . . If you know what Darwin said, you'll be in favor of very gradual change."[4]

Something lingers in the air after we read about Dickey. The facts of the case study, disturbing as they are, do not speak for themselves; there is a surplus of sadness here, something wrenching and cold. Coles is probably right to describe what happens to Dickey in terms of "moral compliance" and the fear of failure. In fact, he is bold to do so: his are not the noncommittal words we have come to expect from a psychiatrist, or from a pastoral counselor for that matter. But the sadness cuts deeper than this. It is about something else, something at once amorphous and all-inclusive, something never mentioned explicitly. Dickey was, for a time, moved by the pain of other children, children he read about and saw on television. He was recruited by their pain and responded to it as best he could. But the forces that bore down on this child stopped him in his tracks. Dickey learned quickly. He learned about subtle dynamics of social compromise and moral compliance. And he learned something else, as well. He began to sense that this is not the kind of world, all in all, that allows a kid to respond to another kid's pain.

"We know something of what true goodness is," H. Richard Niebuhr tells us. We know it because "we recognize goodness in every form of loyalty and love." But our recognition may not be enough. Frankly, we are not sure whether choosing sides with loyalty and love is such a good idea. Niebuhr again: "Our . . . problem is whether goodness is powerful," or "whether it is not forever defeated in actual existence by loveless, thoughtless power."[5] Dickey's lesson came early. He responded and was defeated. He will not be so easily recruited again.

Dickey is not alone in his confusion and sadness. We may speak of God's indifference, or confess that nothing seems to make sense anymore. We may see life through entropic imagery, feeling that things are winding down to nothing in particular. Or we may even see the universe as a hostile and forbidding place.

But Dickey's confusion and disillusionment do not mean that he did not experience a call, an "epiphany of recruitment." Dickey was called. He was drawn beyond himself. He saw and felt something his friends did not. And for a moment he thought he found himself too. An epiphany of recruitment is a significant experience, often remembered and sometimes repressed. It is not mere sentimental reaction or the product of emotional manipulation. The experience is often interpreted as an invitation to see things differently, to live a different kind of life, to embrace one's unique vocation.[6] The events that give rise to these experiences are ordinary enough. They are, more often than not, described as "no big deal."

That's what Martha said when she talked about her visit to an orphanage with some friends. It was no big deal; she didn't know why she always cried when she spoke about it. All that happened was that she was introduced to a young boy from the orphanage and spent several hours with him. They really hit it off. After an hour or so of exchanging pleasantries, and playing with toys, the little boy suddenly turned his face toward Martha's and asked, as if he were asking if she'd ever walked on the moon, "Martha, do you have a daddy?"

Martha's tears were not only for the young boy, of course. She was crying for herself as well, and she knew it. The memory of this encounter stayed with her, seemed to invite her to a different kind of life. Still, Martha had no idea what to do with her invitation. Things as they were at the moment, all in all, just didn't seem to allow much of a response.

WANNA-BE SAINT

If you don't count Ted Williams, St. Francis Xavier was my first hero. In fact, I sensed immediately and not without an edge of sadness that St. Francis, Missionary to the Indies, was more important than Ted Williams and Jackie Jensen combined, perhaps more important than the Boston Red Sox taken as a whole. But in the end, I failed my hero. I got confused about what he was inviting me to do with my young life. Like Dickey, only twenty years earlier, I too decided to back off, at least for a while. Mine was a sacred sadness.

There were approximately seventeen thousand souls in St. Peter's parish when I was a kid, nearly 20 percent of Cambridge's population. For many of them, as for me, the novena to St. Francis was the high point of our sacred calendar. I remember one snowy March afternoon when school had been canceled. We must have had at least a foot of that heavy wet snow characteristic of late winter in New England, and the streets were impassable. I was trudging toward church and the novena when, turning the corner just past Fayerweather Street, I caught sight of hundreds upon hundreds of my fellow parishioners trudging on ahead of me. Many were older, some were very small, and like a holy army they sloshed their way up Observatory Hill to honor St. Francis Xavier, Missionary to the Indies, and to hear his mighty voice raised defiantly, as the hymn put it, "against Satan's wiles and the infernal throng."

I especially liked singing hymns and praying for my special intentions. Concerning the latter, I always prayed, "Please, God, *please* take away my father's arthritis and help Maureen to like me." I prayed about Maureen after I prayed for my father to avoid the appearance of selfishness and did so with a vague sense of the intercessory efficacy of this ordering. As for the singing, I liked the Latin hymns best. They were mysterious, and when we sang them, the wafting clouds of incense carried our words to God and Jesus and Mary and to St. Francis. But my favorite of all was a hymn to St. Francis, which we sang in English. We sang this hymn with great fervor immediately after reciting "The Prayer of St. Francis Xavier" in unison. Looking back, I suspect that it was the beauty and intensity of the prayer, rather than that of the hymn itself, that moved us to sing so enthusiastically:

> O God I love you! I love you, not simply to be saved, and not because those who fail in love to you will be punished with eternal fire. You, you, my Jesus, have all-embraced me on the cross. You have borne the nails, the lance, much ignominy, numberless griefs, sweatings and anguish, and death, and these on account of me and for me, a sinner. Why, therefore should I not love you, O, most loving Jesus? Not that in heaven you shall save me, nor lest for eternity you shall condemn me; not with the hope of any reward, but as you have loved me, so also will I love you— only because you are my King, and because you are my God.

St. Francis died loving Jesus so much that he did not even care if he went to heaven or not. He just wanted to do something for Jesus, who had died for him and for me and for everybody else too. And suffering like Jesus himself, St. Francis Xavier, Missionary to the Indies, was willing not only to die but to bear something awful—maybe worse than dying, my mother explained—called ignominy. I wondered if I could bear the pain of ignominy. There I was with the heathen of the Indies, converting them in droves, thus inspiring the unregenerate remnant to plot my ignominious end. "Yes," I thought, "I'd do that, I think I could do that. I would die in ignominy for Jesus." My heart was on fire as we sang. St. Francis was right—how else could you respond to Jesus' love? How could you not die for him? It would be sad for my parents, but they would certainly be proud of me because their own Brian was a little like St. Francis Xavier.

But martyrdom was not so easily accomplished. It was unlikely that I would be allowed to leave school to become a missionary, and the prospect of enduring years and years of doing whatever it took to become a priest before I could convert heathens and in turn be martyred by them seemed out of the question. I took solace for a time in the fact that communists hated the Catholic Church more than anything. I grasped the implications immediately. The heathens would come to me. If communists invaded America, many would approach the nearest Catholic church to defile the Blessed Sacrament. Remembering that Cambridge is only five or so miles from Boston Harbor, I was encouraged. If I could place myself between the communists and the altar, it seemed likely that I'd be martyred.

But there were other complications. One of them concerned the relation between my financial status and my love for God. Each Saturday morning I received an allowance of thirty-five cents. I remember thinking that this was an odd amount since Peter Paul chocolate almond bars cost a dime each. For this reason I would buy three candy bars on alternate Saturdays, saving the nickel so I could buy four the next week. I occasionally bought a Three Musketeers bar with the surplus nickel, but only because I liked the crisp white wrapper. One week, however, I decided to hoard my money. I was jingling the coins inside my pocket on Sunday morning at St. Peter's when someone from the St. Vincent de Paul Society told us about poor people who didn't have enough to eat and were poorly clothed. I remember crying a little and then feeling inspired to put all of my money into the "poor box." I did.

It came as a great surprise to me that my father regarded what I had done as a mistake. In fact, it was such a bad mistake that he decided that he would not give me any allowance for two weeks. I was hurt, angered, and confused. One thing he said stung more than the rest: "Nobody likes a holy Joe." My father thought I had done something wrong by giving money to poor people. How could that be?

But it was not only money matters that inhibited my full embrace of martyrdom; there was also the matter of "impure thoughts." I confessed them of course, with compulsive regularity and in detail. I can only imagine how I must have bored Fathers Mead, Hanlon, Duquette, Wallace, and so on. Sometimes I eased up a little for fear of scandalizing them.

The familiar measure of the sinfulness of such thoughts was of course whether they had been intentionally "entertained," or merely noticed and released to entice some other unsuspecting parishioner. Truth be told, I was often a willing and cordial host, coaxing these thoughts to stay for dinner and dessert, and perhaps even to spend the night if this were not an inconvenience. I knew that I was forgiven when I left the confessional, usually on a Friday evening, and I would light-step my way home to clam chowder and handfuls of Wise potato chips, before dashing to the living room to watch *Superman*.

Still, I was sad. I was sad because it was clear to me that St. Francis Xavier would never entertain impure thoughts because he loved Jesus more than I did, even though Jesus had died for both of us. It began to dawn on me that I was not worthy to be a martyr, and even if I were, people would say I was just another holy Joe. No more pretending that I didn't care whether I went to heaven or hell either. I cared. It was during this time of sober self-assessment that I twice accidentally decapitated my statue of St. Francis Xavier, Missionary to the Indies, by knocking him off my dresser. The second time, my father refused to glue his head back on, so we threw him out. More blessed ignominy for him and only sadness for me. Maybe I could be a lawyer like my father. People liked him pretty much, and he never seemed bothered by the fact that he wasn't going to be a saint. Still, the sadness remained and remains. I just couldn't love Jesus back like St. Francis Xavier, Missionary to the Indies.

REAWAKENING OUR EPIPHANIES
OF RECRUITMENT

It was 1983, and I'd just arrived in town. "If you want to understand Boulder," a friend told me, "you'll need to make a little pilgrimage to Alfalfa's." So there I was, a week or so later, gawking my way through this first-wave exemplar of a health-food supermarket. I'd never seen the likes of it. Meandering through the aisles, I discovered creamy drinks made from beans and wheat and rice, hairy fruits I couldn't name, herds of free-range chicken, meatless sausage, saltless and fatless (soulless) potato chips in colorless pouches—all this and several dozen variations on trail mix to boot. It was a moment fraught with significance: I wasn't at the University of Chicago anymore. Not that the weight of the place had left me quite yet. I still hadn't completed my dissertation on William James, and he accompanied me wherever I went.

It wasn't the trail mix or the hairy fruits or the free-range chicken herds, however, that came to symbolize that day for me. It was an advertisement—one of those amateur jobs with a fringe of phone-number cut-outs at the bottom of a photocopied yellow sheet—that had the honor. Glancing up at the bulletin board on my way out of Alfalfa's and already slightly dazed from my tour of the place, I read: "Colon Massage Therapy from a Jungian Perspective." I couldn't help but picture what the ad might be adverting to. I also mused as to how colon massage therapy from a Jungian perspective might differ from a Freudian, Marxian, or even a Jamesian perspective. I didn't have a lot to go on.

But what was I to make of such a place? First of all, I had to admit that Boulder was impressive in some ways. Who wouldn't be impressed by the confluence of healthy-minded extroversion, easy affluence, spiritual experimentalism, and unparalleled beauty that defined this place? I also had to admit that I was glad to be in

Boulder. Frankly, another Chicago winter might have done me in.

Still, William James and I were concerned. Was the spiritualized optimism nurtured by three hundred days of sunshine each year, echoed majestically by the Flat-irons glistening at the edge of town, and legitimated by a surfeit of counselors, healers, spiritual companions, and colon massage therapists all that it claimed to be? Did people age in Boulder? Were you allowed to get sick without being blamed for it? Where do they hide the fat folks? The old folks? People of color? Smokers? Baptists?

The more I thought about it, the more I thought that William James would see Boulder as a bastion of healthy-mindedness. He would wonder at the repression of the awareness of the reality of suffering, especially the suffering of those so notably absent from this flourishing community. As impressive as the psychological results of this healthy-minded take on things might be, the optimist's selective and self-interested construction of experience was, for James, a "shallow dodge" and a "mean evasion."

I carried my suspicions of Boulder with me into the classroom. I had been invited by Jack Kelso, director of the Farrand Residential Academic Program at CU-Boulder, to teach a course on the ethical dimensions of leadership. Accepting his invitation, I set out immediately to argue and inspire my new students into admitting that what they really wanted from life was not what they thought they wanted or said they wanted. They wanted something deeper, something better, something else— something William James and I knew was best for them. This something had to do with compassion and with social responsibility, with vocation.

Oddly enough, despite our moralism, despite my woeful inexperience as a teacher, William James and I had a point. The students did seem to desire something deeper, something more idealistic, something different from what they were told constituted success American style. But awakening an exiled shadow government of compassion and idealism is risky business. These young men and women were only too aware of how alienating and constricting were the images of success and failure that the ascendant culture had bequeathed to them. But this knowledge was for many of them accompanied by a sense that they could not afford to look too closely, too systematically, at their own sense of alienation.

Like Dickey, many of them had already tried to live out their compassion and idealism and failed at it. For their troubles, they had been taught the same lesson Dickey had learned so well: it is not realistic to care too much, to feel too much, even to say too much. Like Martha after her experience at the orphanage, many of these young men and women felt a kind of dull pain at the memory of epiphanies of recruitment now grown cold, and they possessed little sense of what, if anything, to do about it. This was a hard lesson.

A former student told me about a particular passage from Douglas Coupland's novel *Life After God*. She thought I might want to copy it for class. She said it reminded her a lot of what we'd said about the exiled shadow government of compassion and idealism, and about Dickey's story too. She lent me the book, and I decided I'd read the whole thing and see if the quote jumped out at me. To be honest, I didn't like it very much. It is unremittingly ironic, sometimes tiresomely so. Nonetheless, when I finally arrived at the quote after an hour or so of reading, I was stung by what I read. Coupland took a break from his irony, from his self-preoccupation, from his game, and said the following: "Now—here is my secret: I tell it to you with an openness of heart that I doubt I shall ever achieve again, so I pray that you are in a quiet room as you hear these words. My secret is that I need God—that I am sick and can no longer make it alone. I need God to help me give, because I no longer seem to be capable of giving; to help me be kind, as I no longer seem capable of kindness; to help me love, as I seem beyond being able to love."[7]

Coupland's words remind me of my commitment to

teach and write in a certain way: one that downplays my original moralism; one that meets the students where they are, rather than where I think they ought to be; one that allows me to admit my own doubts about the possibility of living a different kind of life, even as I take a stand in favor of doing so; one that argues less and listens more and laughs more; one that, above all, is ever-not-yet in terms of where it wishes to lead but is, because of this very fact, somehow already here.

PRACTICE: ASK ME WHAT I'M LIVING FOR

Can Dickey recapture his initial resistance to high-culture racism? Will Martha be able to respond to her moment of recruitment at the orphanage? What of Douglas Coupland's lost capacity for love and kindness? Is my own wanton decapitation of St. Francis Xavier, Missionary to the Indies, an unforgivable act of apostasy? And what about those students who thought Pam was lying about Yale Law School? There's reason to hope for the best.

Consider this passage from Robert Coles's delightful and sometimes woundingly beautiful *Spiritual Life of Children*. The eight-year-old whose epiphany of recruitment Coles records here is young Dorothy Day of Chicago, some thirty years before she found her way to New York's Lower East Side to cofound the Catholic Worker Movement:

> I think my "pilgrimage" began when I was a child, when I was seven or eight. . . . I'm sitting with my mother, and she's telling me about some trouble in the world, about children like me who don't have enough food—they're dying. I'm eating a dough- nut, I think. I ask my mother why other children don't have doughnuts and I do. . . . I don't remember her words, but I can still see her face; it's the face of someone who is sad, and resigned. . . . Most of all, I remember trying to understand what it meant—me eating a doughnut, and lots of children with no food at all. . . . I don't remember my words, I just remem- ber holding the doughnut up and hoping she'd take it and give it to someone, some child. . . . I didn't eat that doughnut! I put it down on the kitchen table. . . . I asked her if God knew someone nearby, or if He could help us with our modest doughnut plan. . . . I don't remember asking her that, asking her how we might enlist God in this effort; but she says I kept talk- ing about God and Jesus and feeding the hungry with doughnuts, until she told me, please, to stop![8]

Did you ever have a doughnut plan? What happened to it? Have you thought about trying it again?

PRACTICE: ASK ME WHAT I THINK IS KEEPING ME FROM LIVING FULLY FOR THE THING I WANT TO LIVE FOR

Should someone who writes a book on ambition wonder whether or not his book might make him a pile of money? I don't know if he should, but I've caught myself doing just that. Ironically, the reason I caught myself is that I decided I'd better engage in a practice I came up with for the class. It's called the "distraction diary." It's pretty straightforward and has proved effective.

Whenever you stop reading unintentionally (neither stopping to make a phone call nor running to the bathroom count as unintentional, though a trancelike walk to the refrigerator might), make a note of whatever it was you were thinking when you first noticed that you were no longer reading. If the unintentional lapse is more than momentary, retrace the conversation as far back as you can and take notes on what you find. The idea here is simply to trick yourself into discovering what you think about, what you're in fact preoccupied with, by catching yourself in an otherwise unmonitored moment of reverie and daydreaming.

I've been recommending this practice for some time, and with good results. Nonetheless, there are some initial questions that need to be addressed. Please play along here and act as though you asked the three questions I'm about to answer.

(1) Yes, doing this activity does make you a little self-conscious at first. You may find yourself distracted from reading by the very fact that you're on the look-out for distractions. That's fine; write it down. This thought itself is, in fact, a distraction.

(2) Yes, of course, it's only natural. You will tend to re-sist this activity, at least at first. Being faced with your actual preoccupations is a little discomforting. They tend not to be as noble as you might wish. Not only that, but you'd probably like to think you al-ready know what your own preoccupations are.

(3) Certainly, I'd be happy to provide a couple of examples.

It may, for instance, feel as though your attention to the text has never wavered. But this often means only that your eyes have kept moving over the page. Some people can continue to read as they daydream and free-associate. You can learn to catch yourself at this pretty easily. Also, you may think that when you stop reading you're some-times completely blank. I don't want to suggest that this is impossible, but it has been my experience that there's always something to jot down. Listen for distant echoes, or for background music.

My own distraction diary grew intricate really fast. Not only did I become adept at catching myself not reading but over time I began to notice patterns of preoccupation that surprised and sometimes embarrassed me. The patterned internal conversations I found over time took on the feel of subpersonalities. So I named them. The Sludge Toad, Ordinary Guy, and the Bird are three of them.

It was the Bird, in fact, who was speaking when I caught a glimpse of him holding a royalty check up to the light. Bird routinely flies off twenty years into the future and tries to make a nest for me out there so that I can feel secure about my retirement years. In fact, more than a few times, I've caught Bird calculating what it would take to retire in ten years and how much more retirement income we'd have in fifteen. Once, I caught Bird pensively eyeing the NASDAQ, though in the end I knew he'd play things pretty conservatively. Discouraged by his calculations and by his skittishness about the market, Bird began to wonder if this book we're working on might not speed things along a little.

I'm not sure whether the distraction diary is the practice for you. Feel free to come up with something else. What's important here is to find a way to become more familiar with your dimly acknowledged preoccu-pations and to do so as gracefully, guiltlessly, playfully, and effectively as possible. There is nothing wrong with playing the stock market or preparing for retirement, or with whatever it is you do that defines your own pre-occupations. There's really no moral problem here per se. But there are spiritual implications to preoccupation: "For where your treasure is, there will your heart be also" (Matthew 6:21).

CHAPTER TWO

Failing at Success

MY DINNER WITH VALENTINO

Each year on the anniversary of his death, a mysterious woman dressed in black places flowers at the grave of Rudolph Valentino. The premature death of the greatest of the silver screen's Latin lovers, on August 23, 1936, threw the country into a state of hysteria punctuated by riots and suicides. Journalists wrote of little else; but no one wrote about Valentino's death in quite the same way as H. L. Mencken, America's most celebrated journalist and curmudgeon. The superiority of Mencken's eulogy is, no doubt, a testimony to his talent as a writer, but it is also a product of synchronicity. A mere week before his death from a ruptured ulcer, a young and apparently healthy Valentino sought out Mencken for advice. Mencken wrote a short essay telling the story of their meeting.

The two celebrities met at a restaurant in Baltimore on a late summer evening so hot, Mencken says, that both men were constantly mopping their faces, first with napkins and then with "the corners of the tablecloth." It was not long after an initial exchange of pleasantries that Mencken found himself wondering what Valentino wanted. It was obvious that Valentino was upset. As far as Mencken could make out, the young actor's problems started when a reporter from Chicago, noting that Valentino used pink talcum powder, blamed him for the increasing feminization of the American male. Predictably, Valentino's outraged response—he challenged his accuser to a duel—only incited his journalistic tormentors and swelled their numbers.

But Valentino's demeanor and the urgency of his tone tipped Mencken off to something deeper and more disturbing beneath this momentary embarrassment: "Suddenly it dawned upon me—I was too dull or it was too hot for me to see it sooner—that what we were talking about was really not what we were talking about at all."[1] Studying Valentino a little more closely, Mencken decided that he was dining with "a curiously naïve and boyish young fellow," a "man of relatively civilized feelings." "It was not that trifling Chicago episode that was riding him," Mencken decided, but "the whole grotesque futility of his life." The lie that festered beneath perceived "success" had been unmasked and had shown its true face: "Had he achieved, out of nothing, a vast and dizzy success? Then that success was hollow as well as vast— a colossal and preposterous nothing. Was he acclaimed by yelling multitudes? Then every time the multitudes yelled he felt himself blushing inside. . . . Imbeciles surrounded him in a dense herd. He was pursued by women—but what women! . . . The thing, at the start, must have only bewildered him. But in those last days, unless I am a worse psychologist than even the professors of psychology, it was revolting him. Worse, it was making him afraid."

Mencken's first take on Valentino is nuanced, sympathetic, empathic. Could it be that Mencken had experienced something similar? Had Mencken written his way into the public consciousness only to ponder the significance of his own "vast and dizzy success"? Perhaps Valentino sensed something of the kind and for this reason sought Mencken's counsel.

But if Valentino was expecting anything more than chatty commiseration, he was sorely disappointed. Mencken kept his thoughts to himself until after Valentino's death. It was just as well that he did. Mencken's journalistic eulogy takes a strange twist as it ends. Unlike his media peers and nearly everyone else in America—in the world for that matter—Mencken did not see

Valentino's premature death as a tragedy. Instead, he was inclined "to think that the inscrutable gods, in taking him off so soon and at a moment of fiery revolt, were very kind to him."

How are we to understand this macabre assessment of Valentino's possibilities? Why would Mencken say this kind of thing about a young man who had impressed him with his sensitivity and gentleness? Was there really no recourse for the young Valentino, no escape from the alienation that was eating away at him, no consolation following his discovery of the emptiness of fame and fortune? Were Valentino's longings for a different kind of life illusory, the product of fear and revulsion and nothing more?

Reflecting on what Valentino would have done had he lived, Mencken claims that he would have tried "to change his fame . . . into something closer to his heart's desire" and in doing so would inevitably have failed. Mencken felt sure that Valentino, following the lead of many another all-too-successful actor, would have chosen "the way of increasing pretension, of solemn artiness, of hollow hocus-pocus, deceptive only to himself." Such a life, in Mencken's eyes, was not worth living. In the end "his tragedy . . . would have only become more acrid and intolerable. For he would have discovered, after vast heavings and yearnings, that what he had come to was indistinguishable from what he had left." In the end, Mencken could comprehend Valentino's desperate longing to embrace a life somehow "closer to his heart's desire" as an invitation to further disillusionment, to more of the same, to despair.

For Mencken, then, there can be no "true success" beyond the "mere success" that Valentino had already achieved. Valentino sought a more solemn and arty script, one that transcended what he had already achieved, a noble script, one that put his heart's desire to words and his alienation to rest. But Mencken thought he knew better. It is all one script in the end, and it is true success that has the bit part.

The notion of true success, American historian Richard Huber tells us, functions as a kind of social release valve: it protects the successful from the resentment of those who fail at mere success. "But what of the [individual] who was a failure?" Huber asks. Wouldn't that person be inclined "to support political radicalism in order to redistribute wealth?" In true success, Huber continues, "the [individual] whose level of achievement fell far below his [sic] level of aspiration could find solace. After all, 'the best things in life are free.'" In true success, the notions of "noble character," "joyful living," and the centrality of family and friends are key elements.[2]

You may wish to condemn Mencken for extending his city-desk toughness to the universe of meaning. But he could hardly help himself. He was, after all, on to something. He intuitively grasped and thought through the social function of true success and the double bind that it implies for the rest of us. If we have come to suspect that a vocational hunch, our vision of true success, is mainly rationalization of our fear of failing at mere success, then what are we to do when, like Valentino and Mencken, we come to see that mere success—our mundane ambitions for fame, power, and fortune—is itself finally empty? No wonder Valentino was frightened.

We are too. Having glimpsed the abyss of meaninglessness, of the futility of pursuing the two-faced illusions of mere success and true success, we are driven to distraction. That is to say, we are thrown back on the social scripts of mere success and to the sad business of hiding our own alienation from ourselves; better alienation than despair. The power of the social scripts of mere success, then, is not, as it is often thought, the power of seduction; it is the power of distraction. We are not, on the whole, greedy and power-hungry to the degree that we are fearful and confused. This simultaneous awareness of both our alienation from the demands placed on us by the pursuit of mere success (our everyday ambitions) and our suspicion that all talk about true success, our vocation or true calling, is mere rationalization can induce paralysis and profound discouragement.

It is this double bind that in part accounts for the taming of Dickey's young passion for social justice, that fuels the fear and suspicion of Pam's classmates, that puts Martha at arm's length from her no-big-deal epiphany of recruitment at the orphanage.

In the final analysis (but is it final?), we often seem to prefer the alienation that accrues from accommodating ourselves to the false consciousness of rigid social roles to the risk of inhabiting a world devoid of meaning and structure. Anomie, sociologist Peter Berger informs us, is a "nightmare world" of "sinister shadows . . . a formless, dark, always ominous jungle."[3] We cannot survive for long in such a world. As a result, we become suspicious of our own longings, our own call. We do not wish to be awakened from the purposeful distraction of chasing stylized images of ourselves in the future.

It may well be that Buechner is right in saying that our vocation, our truest call, is to be found "where [our] deep gladness and the world's deep hunger meet." But it is also the case that we are most vulnerable precisely at such a moment of discovery. This was certainly the case with Dickey.

Perhaps it was the case with Valentino as well. There can be little doubt that he was longing for a different kind of life, a life "closer to his heart's desire." Too bad he looked to H. L. Mencken for guidance. He would have done better consulting with William James, and so, I think, will we.

WILLIAM JAMES AND THE DESIRE FOR SOMETHING MORE

Recall James's quandary, mentioned in the Preface: he wanted to be both a saint and a millionaire but was fearful that what he might do to achieve the latter might disqualify him from achieving the former. James is not alone in this. What are we supposed to do when our ambitions seem at cross-purposes, when our desires for this or that kind of life bump into each other and fall off the track? The whole thing can get pretty complex. In James's case, along with desiring wealth and sanctity, he confesses that he also wants to be "both handsome and fat and well dressed, and a great athlete . . . a wit, a *bon-vivant* . . . a philosopher; a philanthropist, statesman, warrior, and African explorer . . . as well as a 'tone poet.' "[4]

To save himself from a paralysis of action born of limitless possibility, James decided to arrange his various envisioned selves in hierarchical order. If achievement of one seemed to preclude achieving another, or several others, he would simply choose the one of highest rank.

Whatever else he was, James certainly was a success as a philosopher; as such he felt it advisable to both spell out and defend this model of vocational discernment in some detail. As a preliminary step, James distinguishes three types of ambition: material self-seeking, social self-seeking, and spiritual self-seeking. Material self-seeking points to acquisition of wealth and property and a number of other things also. It has its source in the human instinct for self-preservation, manifest in the need for security and material comfort. Social self-seeking is a more complex notion, since each person is constituted by so many "social selves." James observes that there is often a "discordant splitting" among these roles and a resulting wariness of allowing one set of acquaintances to see how we behave in the company of another set. The phrase "club opinion," one that shows up frequently in James's work, gives expression to what he describes as the inevitable desire "to please and to receive the admiration of others." More particularly, social self-seeking points to the power that social groups, what James called "our set," exercise over us when they choose either to "exalt" or "condemn" us. Spiritual self-seeking incorporates not only the dimension we immediately associate with the term—the religious realm of experience—but also the life of the intellect, the aesthetic realm, and the moral life.

For James, if this or that particular element of our material self-seeking conflicts with this or that particular element of our social self-seeking, the material must give way: "We must care more for our honor, our friends, our human ties, than for a sound skin or wealth." If either our social or our material self-seeking clashes with our spiritual self-seeking, we must let go of the former: The "spiritual self is so supremely precious that, rather than lose it," we ought "to be willing to give up friends and good fame, and property, and life itself."[5]

It's a nice scheme all in all, but a scheme that James is not ready to recommend to us without some strong reservations. Self-seeking, even spiritual self-seeking, is after all, well, *self*-seeking, and James notes that all forms of self-seeking tend to cause people "to entrench their Me," and to "retract it." In other words, self-seeking in all its forms appears to be egoistic. Spiritual self-seeking is really no different from material and social self-seeking in that it breeds invidious comparison—that is, comparing ourselves with others in the hope that we are doing better than they are.[6]

But this is problematic: if spiritual self-seeking does not afford a cure for the distortions associated with material and social self-seeking, what can? James saw what

Mencken saw, but he did not draw the same dark conclusion. James would never have discounted Valentino's hope to embrace a different kind of life, one closer to his heart's desire, on the basis of his inability to account for it intellectually. James is too good a philosopher for that.

In fact, James believes there have been actual sightings of people living a different kind of life. James speaks of "sympathetic people" who seem to take a different tack from the self-seekers whose egos entrench and retract: they "proceed by the entirely opposite way of expansion and inclusion." As a result, James tells us, "The outline of their self often gets uncertain enough, but for this the spread of its content more than atones." James's sympathetic people seem to delight in the good fortune of others and be little distressed by their own ill-fortune. They are perhaps better described as self-forgetful than as self-seeking and appear spiritual in a way distinct from those who seek after spirituality: "The magnanimity of these expansive natures is often touching indeed. Such persons can feel a sort of delicate rapture in thinking that, however sick, ill-favored, mean-conditioned, and generally forsaken they may be, they yet are integral parts of the whole of this brave world, have a fellow's share in the strength of dray horses, the happiness of the young people, the wisdom of the wise ones, and are not altogether without part or lot in the good fortunes of the Vanderbilts."[7]

But why does James describe these sympathetic people to us in such detail? What's the point? If we are inspired to emulate them, are we not then simply involved once again in spiritual self-seeking? And if emulation is not the path to such inclusive sympathy, what is? There's no telling, really. James leaves us with his description and nothing more. Perhaps he wishes only to voice a deep longing for something beyond mere self-seeking, for a kind of self-forgetfulness in which we can find rest from the incessant calculation and self-watchfulness entailed in all our competition—material, social, and spiritual.

It is as if James the man has put his arm around James the philosopher and is telling him to take a break. James's internal philosopher does not wish to allow James the man to be set up, to be taken in by false promises. James praises even as he admonishes: "For my own part, I have also a horror of being duped; but I can believe that worse things than being duped may happen . . . in this world. . . . Our errors are surely not such awfully solemn things. In a world where we are so certain to incur them in spite of all our caution, a certain lightness of heart seems healthier than this excessive nervousness on their behalf."[8]

We all have internal philosophers, and it may be that they also need a talking to. Our internal philosophers chatter incessantly, spinning out all manner of hypotheses and pronouncements, and lying, like guard dogs, in wait ready to spring on any would-be solicitor of our passions and of our commitments. These learned guardians of the heart communicate largely by invective, by counterexample, and by implied insult. Our friends do not like them; nor do we much of the time. It is because of them that we refuse a second glass of wine and sometimes need to count to ten before we speak. So why put up with them? We too have a horror of being duped. We are doubly afraid of being duped about things that have to do with the way we live our lives, with whom we fall in love, and to what we commit ourselves. Our internal philosophers do our security checks for us, counsel patience, and advise us to look before we leap—or not to leap at all. Above all, they tell us that if something seems too good to be true, it is in fact too good to be true.

But there is something our internal philosophers cannot afford to know, given their job description. You can miss out on things by waiting too long, by thinking too hard, by floating one too many hypotheses, by confusing grumpy thoughts with intellectual integrity. In trying to protect us, our internal philosophers sometimes talk us out of the deep longings of our heart.

Our longings are facts before they are interpreted. True, they are not untouched by our scripts—material, social, and spiritual—that is to say, we do not experience them unmediated. Nonetheless, Simone Weil, no stranger to philosophy, warns all philosophers, both those on the page and the internal variety, that they are in danger of deceiving themselves if they try to explain away as impossible what in fact is already the case:

> In the period of preparation the soul loves in emptiness. It does not know whether anything real answers its love. . . . The soul knows for certain only that it is hungry. The important thing is that it announces its hunger by crying. A child does not stop crying if we suggest to it that perhaps there is no bread. It goes on crying just the same. The danger is not lest the soul should doubt whether there is any bread, but lest, by a lie, it should persuade itself that it is not hungry. It can only persuade itself of this by lying, for the reality of its hunger is not a belief, it is a certainty.[9]

THE SISTERS OF THE CENACLE
AND HOW TO SNEAK INTO HEAVEN

My own child-hunger for God has less to do with bread than with mashed potatoes, less to do with lying to myself than with the joyous discovery that what I momentarily thought too good to be true was, at the end of the day, too good *not* to be true.

I have a memory from a time before my first acquaintance with St. Francis Xavier, Missionary to the

Indies, a time before I ever aspired to ignominious martyrdom, a time when people took me places whether I wanted to go or not. I would somehow just show up where I was expected to show up and do whatever was expected of me once I arrived.

Every Monday afternoon, I would appear at the Convent of the Cenacle in the Brighton section of Boston. The Cenacle is located on a hill overlooking the Boston skyline not far from Boston College and is, by any standard, a remarkably beautiful place. I took to it from the start. I loved memorizing catechism and talking with older women dressed in a way that showed that they belonged to God. I belonged to God too, even though I wore regular clothes and sneakers. Sometimes I would deliver something to one of the sisters sitting at a big desk in the library. She would whisper "Thank you" and write a return note neatly on a sheet of perfect white paper. The floors were waxed and shiny in the library, and all the books were about God and Jesus and Mary. It was very quiet. I liked being quiet with God and with the sisters. Once I brought a message to the kitchen. You should have seen it there. You could have cooked maybe a hundred turkeys at once and the mashed potatoes to go with them.

One Monday afternoon, we got to have class on the stage in the auditorium. Each week, before going to separate classes, the whole group sang hymns. We always ended with a hymn to Mary. That day, our class didn't even have to move; we just waited for everybody else to leave. Ten of us or so sat around a large folding table clearly meant for adult use. My chin rested comfortably on the table's surface. Michelle, who was very cute and well-behaved, sat directly across from me. It was not long before I discovered that by sliding down the chair ever so slightly I could watch Michelle's tiny pale legs bobbing some two feet above the floor and could on occasion even catch a glimpse of her underwear.

I was not entirely comfortable with this sliding-peeking activity, however, and sensed the incongruity between it and whatever it was that Sister was saying that day. I felt a queasy sense of my own taintedness.

Then something Sister said caught my attention and caused me to sit up a little straighter. I do not recall exactly what she said, but it had something to do with what you needed to do to get into heaven. There was something upsetting about what she said, although I wasn't sure exactly what. It was as if Sister had forgotten that God loved kids no matter what. They told us that before, and I remembered it. Plus, it felt like that in the library, and when we sang "Ave Maria" in the auditorium:

Ave Maria, gratia plena, Dominus tecum,
benedicta tu in mulieribus,
et benedictus fructus ventris tui, Jesus.

53

Sancta Maria, Mater Dei,
ora pro nobis peccatoribus,
nunc et in hora mortis nostrae. Amen.

Hail, Mary, full of grace, the Lord is with you.
O how blest are you among all earth's women.
And how truly blest is the fruit of your
    womb, Jesus.
O holy Mary, God's own mother,
pray for us, your children who stray from the
    way,
now and in that final hour when we come to
    die. Amen.

"But, Sister," I heard myself saying, "don't you think that even if you weren't all that good, God would let you sneak into heaven?" Sister was open to my question, but she stood her ground. I didn't give up immediately, thinking that if I spoke more clearly and slowly, Sister would come around. "But, see, I think . . . you know . . . that God, probably, would . . . um, let a kid, well, sneak in, probably, even if that kid was bad sometimes."

Maybe Sister had been watching me more closely than I thought. I'd tried hard to look attentive, but you never know with them. She thought I was wrong and she told me so. I felt lonely and sad. But soon I was caught up in a daydream.

I was still at the Cenacle, but this time I was dead and remembering that I had not always been very good and knowing that I was not yet old enough to go to confession. I couldn't find the courage to knock on the front door, like some of the really well-behaved dead people. So I went around to the other side and waited at the back door near the kitchen, where I had delivered that message to the other nun. I didn't even have time to knock before God left all the people in the front of the Cenacle near the big white statues and came around to let me in. I was relieved and delighted, but I wasn't surprised. God was really, really happy to see me. "Go into that big kitchen and have some turkey and mashed potatoes with gravy. I'll be right back."

It occurred to me that Sister would be relieved that I'd made it into heaven after all. Michelle was there too. That was good. But there was this other thought I had. I felt it in my belly and in my heart, too: "What wouldn't a kid do for a God like that!"

PRACTICE: REMEMBERING TO FORGET OURSELVES

The Spiritual Exercises of St. Ignatius Loyola, founder of the Jesuits, the Society of Jesus, invite retreatants to carry the defining particularities of their own inevitably broken and graced lives with them into the particularities of a given scriptural passage. Consider, for example, the first chapter of John's gospel, verses 35–38: "The next day John again was standing with two of his disciples, and as he watched Jesus walk by, he exclaimed, 'Look, here is the Lamb of God.' The two disciples heard him say this, and they followed Jesus. When Jesus turned and saw them following, he said to them, 'What are you looking for?'"

What is the weather like? Can you feel the heat on your back? Is there dust in the air? What does John the Baptist look like? What does he sound like? Are you afraid of him? There is Jesus, passing by. John's disciples follow him. He turns . . . He is turning. "What are you looking for?" Jesus says.

So, what *are* you looking for?

■ ■ ■

The following practice is no doubt also inspired by Ignatian spirituality. Anthony De Mello, from whose book *The Way to Love* I have excerpted what follows, was himself a member of the Society of Jesus. Born in India and influenced by Eastern thought and practice, this beloved spiritual director and retreat master died several years ago. You will recognize this exercise as a species of formative remembering in which the author wishes for his readers to remember that forgetting the self is something we long for more ardently and intensely than watching ourselves be successful.

Before trying De Mello's exercise on for size, please call to mind the fact that practice is not technique. To simply follow the steps and hope for the best is to miss the point entirely. For this reason, all practices of self-appropriation should be studied, interpreted, critically evaluated, and finally reconstructed. So let me suggest a particular strategy for approaching De Mello's exercise, one you may find helpful in your own reconstruction of his suggested practice.

First, engage the exercise as De Mello has constructed it, and do so with a cultivated sense of innocence. Try as best you can to bracket your problems, doubts, and inhibitions, be they cognitive, emotive, or unspecifiable. Womanist theorist bell hooks points out a kind of all-or-nothingness about American scholars that I think applies more widely. She notes that as soon as we find an impurity in the water, we refuse to drink it, forgetting for the moment how thirsty we are. De Mello's exercise can be of value if you let it.

Profit and Loss

For what will it profit you, if you gain the whole world and forfeit your life?

—*Matthew 16:26*

Recall the kind of feeling you have when someone praises you, when you are approved, accepted, applauded. And contrast that with the kind of feeling that arises within you when you look at the sunset or the sunrise or Nature in general, or when you read a book or watch a movie that you thoroughly enjoy. Get the taste of this feeling and contrast it with the first, namely, the one that was generated within you when you were praised. Understand that the first type of feeling comes from self-glorification, self-promotion. It is a worldly feeling. The second comes from self-fulfillment, a soul feeling.

Here is another contrast: Recall the kind of feeling you have when you succeed, when you have made it, when you get to the top, when you win a game or a bet or an argument. And contrast it with the kind of feeling you get when you really enjoy the job you are doing, you are absorbed in, the action that you are currently engaged in. And once again notice the qualitative difference between the worldly feeling and the soul feeling.

Yet another contrast: Remember what you felt like when you had power, you were the boss, people looked up to you, took orders from you; or when you were popular. And contrast that worldly feeling with the feeling of intimacy, companionship—the times you thoroughly enjoyed yourself in the company of a friend or with a group in which there was fun and laughter.

Having done this, attempt to understand the true nature of worldly feelings, namely the feelings of self-promotion, self-glorification. They are not natural, they were invented by your society and your culture to make you productive and to make you controllable. These feelings do not produce the nourishment and happiness that is produced when one contemplates Nature or enjoys the company of one's friends or one's work. They were meant to produce thrills, excitement—and emptiness.

Then observe yourself in the course of a day or a week and think how many actions of yours are performed, how many activities engaged in that are uncontaminated by the desire for these thrills, these excitements that only produce emptiness, the desire for attention, approval, fame, popularity, success or power.

And take a look at the people around you. Is there a single one of them who has not become addicted to these worldly feelings? A single one who is not controlled by them, hungers for them, spends every minute of his/her waking life consciously or unconsciously seeking them? When you see this you will understand how people attempt to gain the world and, in the process, lose their soul. . . .

And here is a parable of life for you to ponder on: A group of tourists sits in a bus that is passing through gorgeously beautiful country; lakes and mountains and green fields and rivers. But the shades of the bus are pulled down. They do not have the slightest idea of what lies beyond the windows of the bus. And all the time of their journey is spent in squabbling over who will have the seat of honor in the bus, who will be applauded, who will be well considered. And so they remain till the journey's end.[10]

Next, study De Mello's exercise more closely, noting specifically what factors may inhibit your full engagement. Did you think the disjunction between the worldly and the spiritual is overdrawn, dualistic? Are you angered by De Mello's authoritative, if not patronizing tone? ("Oh yeah, I knew a priest like him when I was in high school.") Did you think to yourself, *If this man of privilege assumes that I've already tasted success to any degree, or that I've been in some wonderful position of power, or God help me that I am in imminent danger of being praised too often and respected too much, it's clear he's from another galaxy! And what's the deal with sunsets? Why do these people always think I should be moved by sunsets?* Or maybe as an astute student of the practices of formative remembering and spiritual indirection you might mumble to yourself, as I have: *The problem here is this practice is too busy: he's trying to do both practices at the same time, trying to have us remember our epiphany of recruitment at the same time he wants us to resist our attachments. It just doesn't work that way.*

Having listed these inhibitive thoughts, and after having taken a short breather, consider the fact that De Mello may be a pretty good fellow after all and that, despite your reservations and flashes of anger, there may actually be something you can learn from him. Ask yourself what De Mello was driving at in the first place, despite the "impurities" of his approach. Review your own dissatisfaction with the exercise and consider what part your own habitual predispositions, opinions, and biases may play in your dissatisfaction. Can you distinguish between your initial reaction to the exercise and your response to it?

Finally, rewrite the exercise. Rewrite it so that it can be of greater value to you if and when you decide to return to it in the future. You may, for example, wish to reconstruct the exercise by noting that the self-consciousness you experience is less about being praised than it is about expecting condemnation, less about gloating over success than dealing with failure again, less about being puffed up by your possession of worldly power than being deflated by your near-complete exclusion from power. (Remember, however, that all self-conscious contemplation of the self in relation to issues of ambition, success, and failure is inevitably the product of having internalized various social scripts and of the specific forms of invidious comparison appropriate to each.) I freely admit the limitations of my own ethnic, class, and gender location. I listen for resistance and I re-formulate as best I can. But in the final analysis, it's up to you to ferret out distortion from your own location.

If, finally, in your judgment this exercise is beyond retrieval, write out why you think this is the case, addressing yourself directly to Anthony De Mello, perhaps in the form of a letter.[11]

TWO PRACTICES: FINDING YOURSELF BY LOSING YOURSELF

If we're going to learn to forget ourselves on purpose without engaging in the contradiction-in-action of chasing after some picture of our future self-forgetful selves, we're going to have to be a little shifty about it. We'll have to try an end run around our own Mencken-like suspicions regarding true success, vocation, or anything else that challenges the mere success of fame, fortune, and power.

De Mello is certainly right to suggest that our moments of self-evaluation are not our most rewarding moments, even when such evaluation comes out on the plus side of the ledger. Still it's not always easy to remember this. So let me remind you again. Unlike De Mello's exercise, the next two (which I often use in the classroom) do not have a religious bearing, though they might by way of courtesy be called spiritual.

Take a few deep breaths, relax your muscles, and find a comfortable sitting position that you can maintain for several minutes with as little motion as possible. In a moment, you'll be reading a sentence without an ending. The idea here is not so much to think up an ending as it is to observe what ending seems to suggest itself. Be especially attentive to images that may arise. It may be helpful to view yourself primarily as an observer of this process, rather than its author. After about five or six minutes of silent time, write or draw some representation of the thoughts and images evoked by the exercise. I suggest you do this quickly, though attentively.

Please read the sentence fragment twice, slowly, drawing out the word *when:* "I will be happy when. . . ."

The second exercise is the same as the first, save the content of the sentence itself. For the second exercise, read this sentence fragment: "I was so happy that time when. . . ."

I have found that responses to the first exercise, "I will be happy when . . . ," are replete with images of lounging, floating, gazing, strolling, and the like. People find themselves sprawled out on huge porches overlooking water, walking contentedly in open fields, bobbing gently on the ocean's surface, transfixed by the sound of the wind in a mountain meadow, sitting down to a Babette-like feast with old friends and loved ones, the wine and conversation flowing freely. Often, a dog tags along for company. The sense emanating from these experiences is one of relaxed openness and unfettered joy.

Responses to the second exercise, "I was so happy when . . . ," are more difficult to sort out and are neither as consistent nor as easily categorized as responses to the first. Still, one particular kind of response is more common than any other. There is considerable talk about being caught up in some kind of activity, being so into something that one loses track of time and pretty much everything else as well.

The first time I tried this exercise, one young woman found herself competing in a golf tournament, "completely lost in her game." Two young men spoke in a similar way about rock climbing. Ultimate Frisbee got a vote, too. One undergraduate surprised herself when the memory of studying for finals, jangled nerves and all, presented itself to her as something painful but really worthwhile. She'd forgotten about herself for a while.

You may notice an experiential feature common to many of the responses to both exercises: the absence of self-defining, comparative self-seeking.[12] By simply remembering how deeply we long for a respite from self-evaluation, our suspicion of true success—that is, of our capacity to extract ourselves from the alienation of conformity to social scripts—can from time to time be circumvented. No one is denying the power of an ascendant social script of success or failure, or that we are all caught up in those scripts to one degree or another. Nonetheless, if we remember that self-evaluation—negative, positive, or indifferent—is just not the whole show, we're a lot better off.

PRACTICE: WHY DO WE DO THAT?

Once a few months ago, on a rainy late afternoon, I was sitting in the car waiting for my wife to emerge from our apartment. It had been a difficult day and I really wanted to just push back and listen to the rain drumming on the car roof. But I also felt a compulsion to turn the radio on, putatively to find out when the rain would end. Maybe I would jog. So I turned the radio on. Then I turned it off. I turned it off before I heard the weather. I listened to the rain for a while.

But why did I divert myself from what I wanted in the first place?

Do you do things at all like that? For instance . . . ?

CHAPTER THREE

Ivan Ilyich, John Dean, and I

How We Deceive Ourselves

DEAN AND ILYICH

In Leo Tolstoy's *The Death of Ivan Ilyich*, the protagonist, a successful lawyer and respected federal judge in Czarist Russia, is a man nearing the peak of his powers, when he is suddenly confronted with the imminence of his own death at the age of forty-five. Months of painful reflection forced on him by his circumstances reveal that the life he had built for himself is a lie, an illusion—a potential life rather than an actual one. The question that tortured him time and again, until it finally coerced him to face the truth about his life, is a variation on the students' concern about how they can discover what they really want: "What if my entire life, my entire conscious life," Ilyich asks himself, "simply was not the real thing?"

But what does Tolstoy mean when he speaks of a life that is "real"? He doesn't say, at least not directly. He simply describes the last moments of Ilyich's life and his sudden deliverance from illusion to reality. As Ilyich thrashed his arms in pain, he unexpectedly caught hold of his son's hand, and immediately his preoccupation with his own pain dissolved. He was delivered from himself and from the unreality of his former life. He would not live to act on this revelation, but the deathbed conversion is enough, and Ilyich's life is redeemed. The story ends powerfully: "Instead of death there was light. . . . 'It is all over,' said someone standing beside him. He heard these words and repeated them in his soul. 'Death is over,' he said to himself. 'There is no more death.' "[1]

We are moved by the beauty of Tolstoy's story, though opinions may vary about Ilyich's deathbed conversion. Perhaps it sets a bad precedent. But what we really want to know is how Ilyich got himself so confused in the first place. Why didn't he know what he really wanted? What was his problem anyway? For Tolstoy, the answer is straightforward enough: worldly ambition is Ilyich's problem. It was Ilyich's fevered attachment to and preoccupation with specific images of success that closed him off to intimations of a better way.

Two clusters of images and events reveal the nature of Ilyich's attachments. The first of these speaks of Ilyich's fascination with the power of his office. The pleasure he derived from his power is the pleasure of invidious comparison, an almost magical sense that in exercising power that diminishes others, the self is somehow enhanced. Of course, Ilyich would not have admitted to such a thing. Perhaps he did not admit it to himself. He was an evenhanded, mildly progressive, and thoroughly professional judge; he saw himself this way and was confident that his colleagues did as well. Yet Ilyich secretly reveled in his power and its potential to control and diminish others. He could call anyone before his bench and see to it that their reputations were ruined. He might even imprison them. The pleasures of invidious comparison were especially sweet when defendants appeared before him in court. "He loved to treat these people courteously, almost as comrades, loved to make them feel that he who had the power to crush them was dealing with them in such a friendly, unpretentious manner."[2]

The second cluster of images concerns Ilyich's social ambitions. If there were anything that could give

Ilyich's life even greater reality and substance than the pleasures of invidious comparison, it would be his acceptance by the social elite of St. Petersburg. He longed for the intoxicating sense of his own significance that easy familiarity with those-who-count would bestow. To this end, Ilyich bought a spacious new home and furnished it with the best of everything: antique furniture, Japanese plates to hang on the wall, new damask draperies, and a footman in a white tie to open the front door. Convinced that his new home had finally achieved an aristocratic air, he sought the opinions of others, who without exception praised its quiet elegance. But Tolstoy (himself a member of minor royalty) wishes us to see through the illusion that Ilyich has created for himself: "In actuality, it was like the homes of all people who are not really rich but who want to look rich, and therefore end up looking like one another."[3]

What is most telling about Ilyich's pantings after social approbation is how quickly he jettisons his former moral code. Ilyich had always regarded his own heavy drinking and occasional philandering as vile behavior. But when he saw "people of high standing" doing such things, though he did not immediately dismiss his own misgivings he felt considerably less perturbed. Soon he was not bothered at all. How could anything be wrong? After all, "it was all done with clean hands, in clean shirts, and with French phrases, and, most importantly, among people of the best society."[4]

Ilyich's strained efforts at achieving a relaxed sense of familiarity with his social superiors seemed to inspire increasing impatience with those he regarded as his social inferiors. Once Ilyich's new home was finished, efforts were made to discourage relatives and former friends, now regarded as shabby, from calling on him. Soon the shabby ones disappeared, and only the best and the brightest kept company with the Ilyiches.

What is to be learned from the fictional case study of Ivan Ilyich? More precisely, what is it that is unmasked? Clearly, Tolstoy, who is unashamedly didactic in many of the short stories and parables written in his later years, wishes his reader to identify with Ilyich's condition, to see that worldly ambition, at least inordinate worldly ambition, leads to moral insensitivity; more important, it gives birth to fundamental confusion about what makes life worthwhile, about what it is that each of us truly wants. The question Ilyich's own soul poses to him is this: "What do you want?" But Ilyich's heart is so painted over by images drawn from the social script, that is, from the ethos of the Russian upper classes and minor royalty, that any response other than the scripted one is unlikely.

But things are not so simple as they might seem. Tolstoy is not suggesting that Ilyich's investment in the ethos of the upper classes and his intoxicated attachment to the pleasure of invidious comparison alone account for Ilyich's self-deception. There is a deeper problem. Ilyich's inability to attend to the voice of his soul has a more willful element to it. Ilyich not only wishes to enjoy the fruits of worldly success but also intends to do so while protecting his own understanding of himself as morally sensitive, of "having lived," that is, as he "should have lived."

In fact, so overwhelming is his need for moral self-justification that even after all is lost—career, power, social approbation—and death is imminent, Ilyich still refuses to consider that he might have lived differently and better. "The voice of his soul" proposes the question to him three times: "What do you want?" The first time, Ilyich is caught off guard but is able to dismiss it as a "bizarre idea." The question is posed more powerfully a second time. Ilyich senses that, were he able to admit his folly, he could surrender peacefully to death. Yet he cannot. The prospect of admitting that his life has not been all it might have been is met with anger and obstinacy: " 'But if only I could understand the reason for this agony. Yet even that is impossible. It would make sense if one could say I had not lived as I should have. But such an admission is impossible,' he uttered inwardly, remembering how his life had conformed to all the laws, rules, and proprieties. 'That is a point I cannot grant,' he told himself, smiling ironically, as though someone could see that smile of his and be taken in by it."[5]

Only the third time that the voice of his soul poses the question to him can he bring himself to consider the unimaginable. He thought that, as he moved closer to positions of power and social distinction, he would also move incrementally closer to happiness. Now he knows better: "It occurred to him that what had seemed utterly inconceivable before—that he had not lived the kind of life he should have—might in fact be true. It occurred to him that those scarcely perceptible impulses of his to protest what people of high rank considered good, vague impulses which he had always suppressed, might have been precisely what mattered, and all the rest not been the real thing."[6]

In addressing the question put to him repeatedly by the voice of his soul, Ilyich offers an answer to what appears to be one of Tolstoy's most pressing questions: "Why didn't Ilyich know what he really wanted, and why don't we?" Ilyich couldn't know because he was caught in a lie, a ubiquitous and all but irresistible lie. Among all of Tolstoy's characters, only Gerasim, who is

a peasant, and Ilyich's young son, not yet fully social-
ized into upper-middle-class proprieties, are not caught
up in it. But the lie is not a simple one; it cannot be identified with the particularities of the social script itself,
the idiosyncratic content of Ilyich's facsimile world. The
lie consists rather in falsifying our internal conversation:
a lie constructed by our strategic inattention.

If Ilyich wished to follow the script of his time, place,
and social class, all the while maintaining a sense of
moral rectitude, he would have to work at it. He would
need to learn what to do with those vague impulses that
called everything into question. He would need to learn
how to repress them, project them, delay them, soften
them, redefine them, ignore them.

It's not easy to adjudicate the inevitable tension between the self perceived as morally responsible and the
self perceived as successful or potentially successful. The
Ilyich case study alerts us to the all-too-human tendency
to repress knowledge of the incompatibility between
these two types of self-perception, or self-regard: per-
ception of the self as morally responsible on the one hand
and as truly successful on the other.

Building on our reading of *The Death of Ivan Ilyich*, and
mindful of Ilyich's recollection of those scarcely perceptible impulses that warned him of his own dissimulation, it helps to offer a metaphor that describes the

nature of these vague impulses that warn of alienation in the midst of growing success. It is the metaphor of a ringing bell. What kind of bell? It might be the *inkin*, a bell used in Zen practice to announce the start of a period of silent attentiveness, or perhaps the tocsin, or alarm bell, that warns of imminent danger.

Though all of us have resilient and impressive skills at redefining a situation to fit our own interests, or better, our perceived and immediate interests, it is also true that each time we invest ourselves in dissimulation, we do so with a degree of dis-ease. We hear a bell ring. We may not think we hear it, or we may hear it and misinterpret it. We may even claim that it is ringing for someone else. Nevertheless, the bell rings. But can we hear it?

Ilyich's tendency toward dissimulation, his willingness to remold moral and spiritual self-understanding to the exigencies of the self perceived as successful, his inattentiveness to the voice of his own deepest longings— all this is familiar enough to each of us, once we pause long enough to take a look, or better to listen, a little more carefully. Still, the capacity of Tolstoy's story to evoke sympathetic identification on the reader's part is limited. We tend to see Ilyich's dissimulation as the kind of thing that other people are likely to do if they're not careful. We do not deny the implications of Tolstoy's classic story for our own lives so much as we keep them at arm's length. When all is said and done, Ilyich remains other, the deceived one who should have known better.

Such is decidedly not the case with the second lawyer called to the stand. In reading John Dean's *Blind Ambition*, many find it easier to identify with the former counsel to President Nixon than with Tolstoy's fictional judge and bureaucrat.[7] Of course, no one much doubts that the bells rang loudly enough for Dean to hear. That time in the park across from the White House, when G. Gordon Liddy gave Dean permission to have him shot if this would help with the cover-up—that was a bell. Then there was the day that he and Fred Fielding (Dean's assistant in the White House Counsel's office) rifled through Howard Hunt's safe, donning surgical gloves to avoid leaving fingerprints. That was another bell. There were many others.

Nonetheless, we are not without sympathy for Dean. We may not excuse him, but we do understand. After all, Dean was barely out of law school when he went to work for the Justice Department and only a little older when offered the new job as counsel to the president. Not only that, but they flew him to the West Coast, first-class; sent a helicopter to fetch him; gave him the rooms at the summer White House usually reserved for John Ehrlichman and family; and even arranged for a conversation with the president. What was he supposed to do?

As the scandal escalated and White House colleagues fell one by one, it is easy to see how Dean—moving ever closer to the center of power—managed to deceive himself into thinking that he was merely a defense lawyer for the whole crew, that he was just doing his job. John Dean did not hear the bells ring. He just had too much to lose. Many of us might not have heard the bells either, or would have attended to them only after we felt too deeply involved to extricate ourselves. This frightens us.

When the two cases are placed side by side, a second metaphor presents itself. It is a metaphor of movement. The first metaphor, that of a ringing bell, calls attention to the tendency to turn a deaf ear to the experiences that warn us of our moral evasiveness. The second expresses the confusion that follows on our evasion. It refers to the confusion (experienced by both Ilyich and Dean) of up with down, and of forward with backward, due to the absence of a moral compass, due, that is, to each man's sometimes willful repression of the felt tension between the self perceived as moral and the self perceived as successful. Dean: "In the Nixon White House, these upward and downward paths diverged, yet joined, like prongs of a tuning fork pitched to a note of expediency. Slowly, steadily, I would climb toward the moral abyss of the President's inner circle until I finally fell into it, thinking

I had made it to the top just as I began to realize I had actually touched bottom."[8] Ilyich: "It's as though I had been going steadily downhill while I imagined I was going up. . . . In public opinion I was moving uphill, but to the same extent life was slipping away from me."[9]

THE ERASER AND THE MENDACIOUS MANTRA

Richard Johnson sat right in front of me in first grade. Richard wore white shirts with dark ink stains on them. Our teacher was Miss Sullivan—not the Miss Sullivan who taught third grade who I had a crush on, who later became managing editor of *Ellery Queen Mystery Magazine*, and who was left-handed and for that reason encouraged me in my own sinisterism, but the Miss Sullivan who was the first-grade teacher near retirement at the time and who had reputedly once pulled down some unfortunate kid's pants and whacked him with a hairbrush and who, worse than that, kept moving my pencil from my left hand to my right. These days, however, Miss Sullivan the elder seemed somewhat less daunting. A harsh but finally ineffectual disciplinarian, she had trouble bringing anyone to justice. It was no secret that Miss Sullivan had trouble hearing; nor were the implications of the fact lost on us. When she turned her back to us to write on the board, she was oblivious to what went on in class.

Richard and I had devised a game. We played it when Miss Sullivan went to the board. The game was called "hide the eraser." Each of us had about half of one of those large gum-colored erasers. They were called Jiffy erasers, I think, and each had the likeness of a knight riding a stallion imprinted on it. I recall being pleased that you could see considerably more than half of the stallion and rider on the half I received.

Anyway, the idea behind the game is obvious enough. Richard would hide the eraser somewhere on his person, or more rarely in his desk, and I would have to guess where it was. There really weren't too many possibilities, and to tell the truth I don't remember whether we played this game for just a few days or weeks or only on this one day. In any case, I was behind in this day's contest. Richard had cleverly hidden the eraser in his shoe or someplace, and it had taken me sixteen guesses to figure it out. I had already challenged both my own and Richard's sense of propriety by hiding it in my underpants in an earlier round—a good inning, by the way—but was now left high and dry.

Then it came to me. It couldn't miss. Brilliant! Richard would never get this one. Who would believe I possessed the courage and skill to stick the eraser up my nose? To my surprise, it fit quite comfortably. That is, it took a little work—anything worthwhile does—but there was a lot more room up there than I expected.

Failing to impute anything from my slightly congested tone as I responded to his queries ("No, it's not inside my right sock" or "No, it's not inside my Chip Hilton baseball novel, or inside my desktop ink-pen holder"), Richard became increasingly frustrated and confused. He guessed dozens of times without success, and I forged into the lead. Finally, as Miss Sullivan turned to write some sort of phonetic formula on the board, Richard turned to me and said, "All right, all right, I give, produce it." He meant by this, of course, that he thought I was lying and that I needed to demonstrate that it was not someplace he'd already guessed. Happy to oblige my vanquished adversary, I delicately placed my middle finger up my nose to retrieve the Jiffy eraser, smirking at Richard triumphantly as I did so. Only, the Jiffy eraser failed to respond properly. In fact, I had the sickly sense that it might even have gone up a little further, drawn by a gentle suction phenomenon of some kind. "Produce it," Richard repeated. "You can't produce it, can you?"

Having no notion of nasal passages, or where they led, I thought that the eraser was moving toward my brain, was already quite near it in fact. Concerned, but thus far fighting off panic, I enlisted my pinky finger, thinking the task demanded a more delicate instrument than I had at first supposed. The results were even worse, and I was sure this time that the Jiffy eraser—stallion, knight, and all—was slowly but inevitably being sucked into my brain. By this time, Richard was a blur and "Produce it, produce it" a distant echo. I was overwhelmed by a sense of cold panic; my life was freeze-framed and my mouth hung wide open. An eraser lodged in my brain suggested terrifying possibilities. One last try resulted in what I most feared: the total disappearance, as I saw it, of the eraser into my brain.

I was terrified, stunned, paralyzed, and, above all, alone. Miss Sullivan would not sympathize. Richard would not sympathize, and my father . . . oh, dear God! But then something occurred to me—a miraculous way out. It came to me in a flash, and I knew just what I had to do. I said firmly to myself and I meant it with all my heart: "This did not happen; it did not happen. I certainly did not stick an eraser up my nose." I felt an immediate sense of relief, despite occasional tremors. I found to my surprise that I could chase away my fears, my shame, by simply repeating my mendacious mantra as often as necessary.

The strategy worked for a couple of days. Unfortunately, the left side of my face began to swell, and one eye closed. So it was off to Harvard Square to see Dr.

Vogel, whom I had always admired, at least until recently, when I heard him call another boy "Chief" as I waited outside his office.

"Take it easy, Chief," he said to me as he peered up my nose with a tiny light. "Say, Chief," Dr. Vogel inquired nonchalantly, "did you stick anything up your nose recently—something pretty big?"

"No, Dr. Vogel, I did not," I replied with conviction and mock confusion. A moment later I was being hoisted onto the examining table. Out came the tweezers, or something like tweezers.

"I've got something here, Betty," he told my anxious mother. "Therrrrre it is." He brought the disgusting thing over to the sink and washed it off. Maybe it was a "growth," I thought. Dr. Vogel had said something about a growth to my mother earlier, and I could tell that a growth wasn't my fault. I held my breath.

"My, my, Chief, what have we here? It's a . . . it's a . . . hmmm? Why, look at that, it's a Jiffy eraser with a picture of a knight on it. I wonder how that ever got up there? Do you think, maybe, they rode up your nose when you weren't looking?"

I was, of course as incredulous as he, as incredulous as my poor mother who looked plaintively into my eyes and said, "But Brian, you've always been such an honest little guy." Ouch.

But all was not lost. After all, Doctor Vogel had "produced it."

PRACTICE: RATIONALIZATION: A USER'S GUIDE

It occurred to Ilyich "that those *scarcely perceptible impulses* of his to protest what people of high rank considered good, vague impulses which he had always suppressed, might have been precisely what mattered, and all the rest had not been the real thing" (italics mine).

On rereading this short passage from *The Death of Ivan Ilyich*, I was reminded of one of the Buddha's discourses, in which he speaks about four kinds of horses: the excellent horse, the good horse, the poor horse, and the really bad horse. Pema Chödrön, a Tibetan Buddhist teacher in Nova Scotia, in explicating the sutra notes that "the excellent horse . . . moves before the whip even touches its back; just the shadow of the whip or the slightest sound from the driver is enough to make the horse move. The good horse runs at the lightest touch of the whip on its back. The poor horse doesn't go until it feels pain, and the very bad horse doesn't budge until the pain penetrates to the marrow of its bones."[10]

Chödrön happily confesses her special affinity with the very bad horse. I'm with her. My own most penetrating insights almost invariably present themselves for

consideration just after I get back on my feet, still dust-
ing myself off after another full-speed collision with yet
another wall.

From the perspective of the Absolute (to continue
the Buddhist idiom), this is just fine, and both Chödrön
and I can take comfort. There is no better or worse in how
we learn what we learn. Zen teacher Shunryu Suzuki,
commenting on the same text, says that the bad horse
actually enjoys a certain advantage: "When you are de-
termined to practice zazen with the great mind of Buddha, you will find the worst horse is the most valuable
one. In your very imperfections you will find the basis
for your firm, way-seeking mind."[11] Some of us, it appears, just pick up the cues, the bells, the emerging signals, those scarcely perceptible impulses a little more
quickly and astutely than others.

With a respectful bow to the worst horse, most of
us think it is a good thing, all in all, to pick up on the
signals, to hear the bells, and do so at least a moment or
two before we run head first into an immovable object,
or feel the whip penetrate to the marrow of our bones,
or find ourselves in jail or on our deathbed. No doubt
there is "more rejoicing in heaven over one sinner re-
penting than over ninety-nine upright people who have
no need of repentance,"[12] but your friends and neighbors, your coworkers and relatives will tend to see things

a little differently. So maybe it would be best to take the initiative ourselves in this matter. Perhaps we can begin with a simple admission and an axiom that flows from it: All of us are very good at rationalizing, and it would be worthwhile to keep this in mind as we make our decisions about work, marriage, and what to have for dinner tonight.

I sometimes tell my students that I am concerned about their limited capacity for rationalization. It's not their ability to rationalize in their written assignments that concerns me; given sufficient time, it is relatively easy to create and defend an experiential falsification of great magnitude. No, my concern is with a kind of stalwart honesty that tends to creep into all too many of our in-class conversations—the kind of damaging integrity that slips out in an unguarded aside, in a gut reaction, in a moment when things bubble up from somewhere we are not familiar with. If you are to be armed for success in the real world, the capacity to rationalize on your feet, extemporaneously and with conviction is not optional; it is required.

First, Meet the Press

You are John Dean's press secretary. You are about to represent Dean in what promises to be a hostile news conference. Reread the Dean segment. List three or four "bells" Dean missed; redefine, reframe, and in short rationalize away the signifying character of these experiences by putting a new spin on things.

I'll prime the pump for you.

PAUL SNIDEFEST, UPI: Ah, Mr. Mahan, we understand that Mr. Dean at one point donned surgical gloves to remove money from a safe in the White House. Can you comment on this? Doesn't this look bad, perhaps even illegal?

BRIAN MAHAN: I have spoken to Mr. Dean about this, Paul, and as you might imagine he is both embarrassed and concerned. Mainly, he's embarrassed. [Uneasy laughter.] It may seem odd, on first appearance, Paul—and I understand that—but Mr. Dean's deepest motivation was to save the White House, and for that matter the American people, any further embarrassment about this whole unfortunate episode. His donning the gloves in question was—oh, and, Paul, they were actually not surgical gloves per se but, strictly speaking, these were the type of gloves routinely used for, ah . . . testing for prostate problems and—but what I'm saying is that the wearing of these gloves testifies not to Mr. Dean's moral insensitivity but to his hypersensitivity around issues of this kind, these moral and ethical issues.

Mr. Dean is aware of the necessity of not only behaving properly in such matters but also avoiding even the appearance of impropriety. If fingerprints had been found on those documents, especially his own—remember, Mr. Dean is the president's lawyer—it would have been hard to avoid the appearance of impropriety, despite Mr. Dean's perfectly legitimate motivations in the matter.

NADINE SLIGHTMEYER, *BOSTON GLOBE:* Mr. Mahan, when G. Gordon Liddy said, for want of a better phrase, that he was willing to have Dean "take him out," didn't Mr. Dean sense that perhaps things were getting a little out of control? That he ought to bring this to the president or someone else in authority?

BRIAN MAHAN: Ms. Slightmeyer, have you listened to Mr. Liddy's talk show? He advertises calendars featuring seminude women holding firearms as a great Christmas gift. He did a lecture tour with Timothy Leary, for God's sake. He has taken every opportunity to denigrate Mr. Dean's character and impugn his motives. He brags about being able to kill with a pencil, and he likes to hold his hand over a flame for entertainment purposes.

I just don't think it's all that farfetched to say that Mr. Dean had written Mr. Liddy off before that bizarre encounter. Mr. Dean, remember, did not hire Mr. Liddy and had little in the way of control over his actions, let alone his words.

You get the idea. Have fun.

Then, Face the Nation

Recall some situation in your life (perhaps it concerns a relationship gone bad, or some regrettable decisions you have made at the workplace) where you are ready to admit that you engaged in acts of self-deception with some frequency.

Next, take some time (I am speaking here of hours rather than minutes) to review the emerging signals, the bells, to which you turned a deaf ear at the time. (It may be best to work backward, first studying your present public stance on the events in question and then moving back a step at a time.) Attend to the echoes of these experiences as they reverberate in your memory. Doing your utmost to put aside any guilt, embarrassment, or shame, try to cultivate a sense of curiosity about the particulars of your techniques for ignoring the bells. What were your favored avoidance techniques? Are they still in play? Are there friends or relatives who can help you with this practice by reminding you of particular events, words, and actions you'd rather not hear about?

Finally, hold your own press conference. Ask tough questions. Drawing on what you've just learned, write out your grade-A rationalizations in response. Study them. Look for patterns in your responses.

CHAPTER FOUR

If I'm Really Something, You Must Be Nothing Much

A SHORT TIRADE

Frankly, I often wonder about our culture's lionization of ambition. I suppose it's all right to sprint after whatever it is we really want, to pursue it with tireless diligence and great passion. But one fact diminishes my would-be enthusiasm considerably: few if any of us seem to have a clue about what it is we really want.

When we speak of the "virtue" of ambition itself, as our culture often does, we usually speak in gross and evasive generalities. We point to a vague something that translates into an even vaguer sense that someone "has what it takes." But this someone who has what it takes, who has the right stuff, has it to get what? to achieve what? to be what? We assume, it would appear, that each of us can fill in the blank for ourselves. We'll just scribble in something later.

We do whatever it takes to avoid admitting that our ambitions come to us already scripted, complete with instruction manual. We think of ambition as a kind of dynamic power or force field. Ambition is simply "the fuel of achievement,"[1] and what direction we take and what our destination may be are entirely up to us. If we desire fame, wealth, and power, well, that's what we desire. But others have ambitions for world peace and inner harmony, and that's all right too. Ambition is whatever we make of it.

But this is nonsense. It is closer to the truth to say that we are what our ambitions make of us. There is no such thing as ambition in general. Desire in its raw specificity is always *for* this or that. It is only later that we abstract from these particulars and speak in tame generalities. The raw imaginal and emotionally charged particulars of what we evasively call wealth or power or love or compassion are what beckon us, thrill us, deceive us. Ambition in general is a nullity; ambition in its specificity may come to define our lives.

Why do we call ourselves individualists and yet congratulate each other for wanting pretty much the same things out of life as everyone else? How can we read incessantly from the same tired scripts, believing for all the world that each of us has written our own in isolation, explaining away the inevitable similarities among them as evidence of shared genius or spiritual kinship? I mean, haven't we already seen enough? What do we make of the radical distrust of a twenty-one-year-old whose only sin was to choose the Peace Corps over Yale? Why aren't we angered by the coerced moral surrender of a twelve-year-old to his already fatalistic peers and mentors? And what of Ivan Ilyich's secret savoring of his power to ruin the lives of friends and acquaintances and of John Dean's intoxicated blindness to the implications of his own ambition for an entire nation?

In American society, in part because of our accent on egalitarianism and our antipathy toward inherited class structure, individual achievement is supremely important. In itself, this is neither good nor bad. It is merely part of the script. The trouble is that it becomes difficult to assess achievement and monitor happiness without surrendering to the impulse to adopt invidious comparison as a prime measure of individual worth. Some invidious comparisons are harmless enough, and many are, in any case, unavoidable. We take standardized tests, get accepted or rejected by various degree programs, accept a job that someone else does not get, and lose a promotion that goes instead to a colleague.

But there is a darker side to invidious comparison. It is the dirty little secret of our society, and we all share in the effort to keep it under wraps. We all know the dark conversations of our hearts, if only intermittently and selectively, and most of us choose to keep them to ourselves. Unfortunately, not everyone can keep a secret. Thomas Merton, in the quiet of his cloistered cell, was attentive enough to hear the darker voice of invidious comparison echo in his solitude. In spelling out his thoughts, he confronts us with our own: "I have what you have not. I am what you are not. I have taken what you have failed to take. . . . Therefore you suffer and I am happy, you are despised and I am praised, you die and I live; you are nothing and I am something."[2]

Our ambitions and the sentiments attached to them are harmless enough when viewed in their sanitized, abstract, daylight visage; but in their raw specificity, they are something else, something darker, something we do not wish to see or, having seen, do not wish to remember. Merton's thoughts are vicious, annihilating, murderous. But this Trappist speaks less from guilt and shame or from the compulsive need to confess than from the authority of one committed to self-discovery in a way that most of us must avoid at all costs.

Do we really want to discover these kinds of things about ourselves? What's the payoff? Perhaps it would help to amend this moral diatribe with an appeal to rational self-interest. What if the pursuit of our ambitions in their idiosyncratic particularities is an absurdity?

Let me begin with a rhetorical question: What are we thinking when we set out in hot pursuit of some socially scripted, envisioned self? What we think we're about is best pictured as a quixotic search for a series of increasingly unlikely events leading nowhere and signifying nothing. Here is the sequence. We first form some elements of our assigned social script into a vastly improved future self. We next crumple it up into a ball, toss it out into the future somewhere, and sprint after it with wide-eyed anticipation, believing all the while that when we finally catch up with it again we will have achieved happiness or peace or some reasonable facsimile.

But how is it that we expect to catch up with our envisioned selves? Really, the whole thing is impossible from the start. Think about it. In the first place, this envisioned self we pant after is not out there. It resides, if it can be said to reside anywhere, in our imagination as a vital but volatile element of the available self; for that very reason it exists in a whirlwind of change, redefinition, and instability. The congruence we seek—the matching up of some self that exists now with some self that exists off somewhere in an ideal future—is an illusion, albeit an immensely popular one. Realizing our ambitions is more like trying to achieve and maintain a state of ongoing and dynamic congruence with a series of kaleidoscopic images of rapidly alternating colors, shapes, and sizes. Our ambitions just won't stand still.

This is not all. Even if we grant the possibility of achieving such an unlikely congruence, there is another problem. We project not only images of our envisioned selves into a fictional future but also, along with them, our expectations of how we will feel when this impossible dynamic and ongoing congruence is achieved. "When that day comes," we muse, "I'll finally have some peace of mind." Or we think, "I'd be in something like a permanent state of exhilaration and excitement, if only I could achieve, experience, or attain such and such or be like or better than so and so."[3] It would appear, then, that realizing our ambitions requires the achievement of not one but two distinctly impossible full-speed kaleidoscopic congruences, in perfect synchronization.

But there's more. These twice-impossible full-speed simultaneous kaleidoscopic congruences are themselves fragile structures, dependent for their emergence and longevity not only on our skill and acumen but on the full and perfect cooperation of the rest of the universe. Our own health, that of our loved ones, the iffy circumstances of international relations, and the vagaries of the weather and the stock market need to be monitored and controlled if we are to get any payoff from having finally caught up with our envisioned self.

And what if, putting all this aside, it comes to pass that we achieve and maintain some unheard-of consonance between the now-self and the then-self? Will we be satisfied, at peace, ready to call it quits? Probably not. Robert Nozick posed just this question to himself, asking how it would be if he achieved "the most exalted and far-reaching life or role imagined" for a human being (at least from the viewpoint of a brilliant and irreverent Jewish philosopher): "being the messiah." "Greater effect" could hardly be imagined, he says. "Yet still we can ask how important it is to bring whatever it is the messiah brings to the living beings of the third planet of a minor off-center star in the Milky Way galaxy . . . one of many in the universe."[4] There is, then, no real end point for our ambitions and no place to rest. So what's the point?

Given all this, might it not be best just to deny, repress, or otherwise expunge our ambitions for fame, wealth, and power, as well as our kindred aspirations toward moral sensitivity and spiritual depth, and move on to something better?

But it's no use, really. Rational argument and moral exhortation are simply overmatched, out of their league, beyond their depth. If we insist on chasing the illusions of the someday self into the sometime future, it is because we need to do so, because we cannot do otherwise. We are distracted and consoled by our little games, perhaps necessarily so. Why else would we be so insistent in our pursuit of what cannot ever be? Nietzsche is correct when he says that we "would sooner have the void for [our] purpose than be void of purpose."[5] We are not about to hand over our illusions, nor should we. We cannot look at things as they are, whatever that phrase might mean, or allow the press of untamed experience free access.

Our self-defense, our games, our ego are deployed not only against the cosmic night—that is to say, against meaninglessness. They are deployed also and perhaps even more vigorously against the terrifying surplus of creating and decreating Love that permeates the universe, painfully reshaping all things to the contours of Its own Image: "But if God speaks to us we will die."[6]

■ ■ ■

Well, I've made my opening arguments about the vanity of worldly ambition. But now, like a lawyer chastised for improper tactics, I withdraw my arguments and nod in agreement as they are struck from the record. And like that lawyer chastised for improper tactics, I also hope something of this might stick, even as I adopt a better, less coercive approach and apologize profusely for my poor behavior. It is now time to examine the evidence in more detail.

THE HIDDEN FOUNTAINS AND GARDENS
OF THE HEART

We humbly confess ourselves sinners and resolutely deny all the particulars. It's the same with our attachment to wealth, fame, power, and the rest. We know our lives are scripted and that the scripts have to do with such things, but we'd rather leave it at that. True, the particularities of Dean's and Ilyich's scripted "programs for happiness"[7]—Porsches and servants with white gloves, an office closer to the president's, damask draperies—add substance and color to a case study. But they do not transfer well. We don't easily see the scripts at work in the particularity of our own self-seekings.

Many of us gladly listen to sociologists and anthropologists and psychologists and sometimes even to philosophers and theologians who speak about such things in their own characteristic way. In fact, some of us learn to employ their terminology with alacrity and sophistication—social context, class location, mediated meaning, blind impress, ethos, concupiscence. We may even come to extol the relevancy of such notions to everyday life—again, in a general sort of way. Some of us become adept at extracting subtle elements of social scriptedness from the posturing of our political and ideological adversaries and at uncovering the hidden motives of friends, colleagues, and loved ones who have fallen into error (as we see it).

It is for this reason that making the transition from unmasking the scripted illusions of others in a case study to doing the same for ourselves is so difficult. In fact, this move to unmasking our own illusions in their particularity—that is, to asking what is keeping us from living fully for the thing we want to live for—is the most difficult and crucial element of the practice of spiritual indirection. More than once I have succumbed to the temptation to run from this challenge and settle for something less, justifying my reluctance with claims of humility ("After all, all I can do is lay out case studies and a little theory and hope that the personal implications are apparent"). But I know better. It is important to provide an escort for bookish insights as they move toward the heartland of self-reference.

The Dean and Ilyich stories demonstrate that blind adherence to the plain text of these scripts—that is, to the uncritical pursuit of power, wealth, and fame—often leads to personal alienation as well as to diminished capacity for compassion for others. But these insights carry us only so far. They are not, in and of themselves, self-referential. The question is, how can we be encouraged and empowered to take the first step toward unmasking the idiosyncratic particularities of our own unadmitted attachments? How do we catch ourselves in the act of chasing after our prefabricated envisioned selves?

But you and I are not the only ones to keep the self-referential implications of the case studies at arm's length. Martin Heidegger, that most redoubtable of twentieth-century metaphysicians, did the same. He saw what Tolstoy was driving at in *The Death of Ivan Ilyich*, and the story influenced his own classic, *Being and Time*. His concepts of "evasive concealment" and "tranquilized everyday-ness" grow in part out of his reading of the story. But Heidegger's cosmic appropriation of Tolstoy never touches ground. His own ambition games, his ideal-ization of the Germanic tribe and language, his role in policing the academic suitability of his colleagues in a context saturated by lethal anti-Semitism, were granted immunity from introspective analysis. Does this mean that we ignore Heidegger as a philosopher? No, it does not; but that's not the question here. Heidegger's case demonstrates that a thorough and subtle reading of Tolstoy's classic may still manage to translate itself in-to magnificent abstraction without ever really hitting home. One philosopher claims that Heidegger "univer-salizes" the themes he finds in *The Death of Ivan Ilyich*. True enough and a good thing too; otherwise, the story might have ended up having something to do with Martin Hei-degger.

Our own willingness to learn from the lessons of Dean and Ilyich and others is limited by our investment in our own attachments—that is to say, by our closely guarded and cleverly concealed "programs for happiness." So Heidegger is at once deceived and true to the mark in his universalizing impulse. But the particularities of our deception cannot be brought to light by consenting, however vigorously, to a correct generality about the human situation or by limiting our consideration to the text itself. If a case study strikes a little too close to home, we either seek cover in the density of the particular ("This story is about this deeply deceived fellow from St. Petersburg who had to face the music once he found out he was dying of a 'floating kidney' ") or alternatively we go cosmic, propelling ourselves away from insight about the particularities of our own life at warp speed ("Tolstoy's Ilyich stands for the inevitability of self-deception, for the blindness of our species, for just about anything that sounds edifying and floats around without lighting anywhere").

If my programs for happiness are at all like Ilyich's, if they involve projected images of my acceptance by a social elite as well as the material trappings associated with such, I will probably want to rationalize as Ilyich does, keeping my distance from him at the same time: "The doorman with white gloves is a little much, I can see that, but the antiques, the Japanese plates, and the damask draperies are harmless enough. But really, I think it's a little far-fetched for Tolstoy to claim that these innocent attachments to beautiful things had anything to do with Ilyich's banishment of the shabby ones who did not fit with the decor or with his inexcusable disdain for defendants who came to his court frantic about their fate."

Look at John Dean. "You're not telling me," you might object, "that Dean's social and material self-seeking encoded within such things as a Porsche, scotch and water, a private helicopter, tennis with the vice president, an office closer to the president's, batting the breeze with the big boys in the Oval Office in knee-trembling proximity to incalculable power could in part account for Dean's moral deafness?" But what else can we think, given Dean's reaction on August 29, 1972, when President Nixon lied to a national television audience, claiming that "Mr. Dean has conducted a complete investigation of all leads . . . [and] I can say categorically that his investigation indicates that no one in the White House staff, no one in this Administration . . . was involved in this very bizarre incident"? Dean said to himself: "How about that? The President was mentioning my name! On national television. *That*, I thought, was a real vote of confidence. . . . I had never been certain the President even remembered he had a fellow named Dean as his counsel, given the negligible contact I had with him."[8]

To repeat: when the personal implications of the story hit too close to home, we're going to try our best to write them off. We're going to protect ourselves, after all.

Despite all our precautions in such matters, most of us nonetheless manage an insight here and there. Sometimes a playful sense of the inevitability of our idiosyncratic attachments to all kinds of things takes hold of us, moving us to confession and commiseration, and even to laughter or tears.

A couple of years ago, I found myself face to face with surprisingly evocative images of my own thinly cloaked social and material self-seeking. I was teaching "The Ethics of Ambition" as an adult education class for the first time. Seven or eight of us were sipping tea in the downstairs classroom of the Aquinas Center, the Catholic theological center here at Emory. We'd been talking about John Dean and Ivan Ilyich when I wondered out loud if anyone could come up with similarly evocative images of the kind that had hooked Dean and Ilyich, adding playfully that it would be particularly appreciated if anyone could link these invested images to their own inexcusable insensitivity to others. I was surprised by the quickness of one woman's response and by the power of what it evoked in me: "Well, yes, that damned fountain for one thing. My friend was moving back to Atlanta—one of my best friends. And I was so happy she was coming home.

I was ready to see her big house and all. I was not going to be jealous. I knew she had money, and that was fine. But when I saw that fountain in her front driveway—water splashing and bubbling everywhere and spilling onto her circular driveway—I was jealous, and I gave her a hard time, a really hard time all day. I wanted to hurt her."

What that fountain triggered for this young woman is hard to say. She was not sure herself. But it set off something in me. As she spoke, I found myself thinking about my copy of *Hidden Gardens of Beacon Hill* with its evocative depictions of red brick, ivy, diminutive statuary, the echoes of the author's commentary describing the Hillier garden (my favorite): "With a discerning eye, the new owner chose to retain its most attractive features: the established beds of English ivy, the fine old hydrangea twining its way up a tall ailanthus tree, and the treatment of the rear wall with redwood window boxes below a picket fence. . . . The distinctive French wire furniture was discovered in an antique shop in Maine: 'What I like about these pieces is their lacy, airy quality. They are a bit whimsical, but formal as well, and on a sunny day they cast beautiful shadows on the bricks.'"[9]

Next class, I brought the book in and passed it around. I found myself speaking about all kinds of things

I associated with it: the Isabella Stewart Gardner Museum, passages from J. P. Marquand in *The Late George Apley* and from Santayana in *The Last Puritan*. That voice, the one I heard reading from *Hidden Gardens of Beacon Hill*— that voice, I told them, was predominantly, though not entirely, the voice of William Pierce of WCRB and the Boston Symphony. There was a memory of shaking hands with my father's friend, the stately governor of Massachusetts, the Hon. Christian A. Herter, and another of Elliott Richardson when he stood his ground against Nixon. The images clustered and mixed, and I spoke about whatever came to mind.

Now I was telling them about Mrs. Spencer, who my mother said "was in the 'Blue Book' but did not put on airs." Mrs. Spencer took an interest in a ten-year-old Irish-Catholic kid who sprinkled peat moss on her beautiful garden on Lake View Avenue, just off Brattle Street. Mrs. Spencer had inherited her furniture and her friends as well, and she tutored young women in French. In our last conversation, twenty years later, sometime in the late seventies, she said she was gratified to hear that I'd gone to Harvard Divinity School (though of course she knew I would because I always stared off into space when I should have been spreading peat moss). I told her that I was writing my dissertation on William James.

"Was he the thin one or the chubby one?" Mrs. Spencer wanted to know.

"He was the thin one, Mrs. Spencer."

The garden was beautiful that day, and we had lemonade and cookies as before. God bless you, Mrs. Spencer. And there I was, tears welling up, in front of class.

It surprised me. There are other Boston images, more immediately accessible, that I'd be more likely to tell you about: Tip O'Neill shaking hands and mingling amiably with a crowd in North Cambridge; John F. Kennedy passing through Harvard Square in a black limousine; my grandmother's wake and the anonymous storyteller who showed up there and talked about John L. Sullivan and Mayor James Michael Curley and the day President Coolidge rode through the neighborhood; white women shouting things at black children and throwing rocks at a bus; and someone repeating the rumor that Tom Mahoney had become an Episcopalian, "so now you can't vote for him anymore." (I thought to myself, "But Tom Mahoney would never do a thing like that.")

But Mrs. Spencer hurt my feelings once. She told me that her husband was "from the wrong side of the tracks."

"But he went to Harvard, Mrs. Spencer."

"That doesn't mean anything," she said.

"What about Catholics?" I asked.

She said Mozart was a Catholic, but she knew what I meant, and she was uncomfortable, and I knew she felt sorry for me.

Do I remember the Big House in County Roscommon[10] and find it again on Brattle Street? Did revolutionary colonists or neocolonials compile the Blue Book? Do I still carry unremembered terror and shame of the Potato Famine even as culpable heir to the legacy of slavery? There's a lot to unpack here. Some of the images and feelings I know fairly well; others remain hidden. On the face of it, I'd rather be a friend of Eddie Coyle's, ride shotgun with Spenser and Hawk, assist Cuddy on his next case.[11] But the tough Irish detective and the Irish missionary to the Indies are relational and reactive characters more than I'd like to admit, a strategy of consolation and defiance as much as anything else, a buttress against obscurely intense expectations from the hidden gardens of the many flowerings of New England culture.

I think it's the images that we don't talk about, don't catch, don't echo and inspect that are likely to have a hold on us, to dictate our decisions, determine our moods, and desensitize us to our daily recruitment by neighbors near and far and by God as well. The hidden fountains and gardens of the heart are the deeper wellsprings of our striving and longing. I wonder what I might do or neglect to do to realize the repressed imagery and all that it stands for of a late summer's afternoon in the beautiful Hillier garden—no, in the beautiful and tasteful Mahan garden just off Beacon Hill:

"I'm not sure; did I tell you that I discovered this distinctive French furniture in an antique shop in Maine? What I like about these pieces is their lacy, airy quality. They are a bit whimsical but formal as well, and on a sunny day they cast beautiful shadows on the bricks. Please sit down. Can I get you something? Maybe I could tempt you with some of these cookies and a little lemonade."

PRACTICE: WALKER PERCY AND SPIRITUAL INDIRECTION

It was seven hundred years ago that Zen master Dogen, one of the greatest spiritual masters the world has known, noted that "to study the self is to forget the self, and to forget the self is to be enlightened by the ten thousand things." But how do we study the self? How do we forget the self? And wait a minute: Isn't studying the self the very antithesis of forgetting the self? You wouldn't teach a centipede to walk by telling it to watch its feet, would you?

But that's not the kind of thing that Dogen has in mind. When Dogen speaks about the study of the self, he is not recommending a state of mind and heart that interferes with doing whatever it is we are doing at the moment. In fact, he means quite the opposite: Dogen is recommending that we study precisely those elements of the self that interfere with what we're doing, that inhibit us from just doing whatever it is we are doing at the moment. Without claiming the authority of Dogen for what follows, I would like to suggest that practicing spiritual indirection invites a similar forgetting of the self through studying the self.

Our inspection of the idiosyncratic specificity of the fountains and gardens of the hidden self represents a good first step. Let me now enlist the help of Walker Percy and his wonderful spoof on self-help literature, *Lost in the Cosmos: The Last Self-Help Book*,[12] to carry things a little further by putting an unmistakably Western spin on this profound Eastern insight.

One of Percy's favorite devices is the multiple-choice test. Percy mimics perfectly the format you would expect to find were you breezing through a magazine looking to improve your fashion IQ or put new zest in your love life, or were you searching for tips on how to dress for success. It is not long before we see that deeper questions about the self and its habits, attachments, deceptions, fears, destiny, and bewildering complexity are this author's chief subject matter. This particular exercise

has as its object to study those attachments and preoccupations that limit and blunt our capacity for compassion. In Dogen-like fashion, Percy's exercise suggests
that if you wish to be compassionate, study why it is that
you are not compassionate.

So please clear your desk, pick up your pencil, and
begin when you are ready.

You are standing by your paper-tube in Englewood
reading the headlines. Your neighbor comes out to
get his paper. You look at him sympathetically. You
know he has been having severe chest pains and is
facing coronary bypass surgery. But he is not act-
ing like a cardiac patient this morning. Over he jogs
in his sweat pants, all smiles. He has triple good
news. His chest ailment turned out to be a hiatal her-
nia, not serious. He's got a promotion and is moving
to Greenwich, where he can keep his boat in the
water rather than on a trailer.

"Great, Charlie! I'm really happy for you."

Are you happy for him?

(a) Yes. Unrelievedly good news. Surely it is good
news all around that Charlie is alive and well and
not dead or invalided. Surely, too, it is good for him
and not bad for you if he also moves up in the world,
buys a house in Greenwich where he can keep a 25-
foot sloop moored in the Sound rather than a 12-foot
Mayflower on a trailer in the garage in Englewood.

(b) Putatively good news but—but what? But the trouble is, it is good news for Charlie, but you don't feel so good.

(CHECK ONE)

If your answer is (b), could you specify your dissatisfaction, i.e., do the following thought experiment: which of the following news vis-à-vis Charlie and you at the paper-tube would make you feel better:

(1) Charlie is dead.

(2) Charlie has undergone a quadruple coronary bypass and may not make it.

(3) Charlie does not have heart trouble but he did not get his promotion or his house in Greenwich.

(4) Charlie does not have heart trouble and did get his promotion but can't afford to move to Greenwich.

(5) You, too, have received triple good news, so both of you can celebrate.

(6) You have not received good news, but just after hearing Charlie's triple good news, you catch sight of a garbage truck out of control and headed straight for Charlie—whose life you save by throwing a body block that knocks him behind a tree. (Why does it make you feel better to save Charlie's life and thus turn his triple good news into quadruple good fortune?)

(7) You have not received good news, but just after you hear Charlie's triple good news, an earthquake levels Manhattan. There the two of you stand,

gazing bemused at the ruins across the Hudson from Englewood Cliffs.

(CHECK ONE)

In a word, how much good news about Charlie can you tolerate without compensatory catastrophes, heroic rescues, and such?[13]

■ ■ ■

Note, first of all, that Percy calls the foregoing a "thought experiment." He does not ask which imagined state of affairs we wish to occur, only which most appeals to our imagination. Percy is neither celebrating nor condemning the dark impulses of the human heart already unearthed for us by Merton and Tolstoy; he is simply inviting us to do what they did: catch them, study them, and by way of indirection move past them. He is pointing to the secret fountains and gardens of our inner life; he is flushing them out of their hiding place; and he is teasing us, good-naturedly enough, into admitting how we've often provided them with cover and a credible alibi. Percy, then, like Tolstoy, is aiming beneath the surface of things, beneath the public persona that hides from both self and others the images that sketch the secret desires of the human heart.

Percy, again like Tolstoy, means to demonstrate that ambitions, yours and mine, in their idiosyncratic specificity inhibit compassion by setting limits on the reach and intensity of fellow-feeling. Perhaps it is the image of the yacht bobbing gently in some Connecticut harbor that gets to us, causes us a slight pang of resentment, thus diminishing our capacity for celebrating Charlie's triple good news. Or maybe it has more to do with our sense that Charlie is jogging around in his tasteless orange spandex, secretly savoring an invidious comparison at our expense.

But unlike Tolstoy, Percy does not treat these newly surfaced attachments as unmitigated lies. Socialization into the ascendant success scripts and the symbols that embody and celebrate them—yachts, new ZIP codes, and the rest of it—is less scandalous, less damning for Percy than it is for Tolstoy. Feeling a twinge of jealousy and a measure of resentment in some obviously scripted way because a neighbor is passing us by is just the kind of thing people are likely to do.

In fact, it is Percy's special genius to recognize and to point out gently that attachment to scripted images of the self as already moral—that is to say, as already beyond such petty jealousy and attachment—is more likely to inhibit practices of self-discovery than to encourage them. Paradoxically, it is the simultaneous confession and careful study of our sometimes conflicting attachments to material, social, and moral scripts that hints at the possibility of joyful detachment and of a life given over more fully to vocation. If you wish to forget the self, study the self. If you wish to be compassionate, study how you are not compassionate.

In summary, Percy's exercise whispers to us in that open space of the heart when we are suddenly, though perhaps only momentarily, willing to take a good look: "Aren't we an odd bunch, you and I and the rest of them, too? I wonder what we can do about it. I wonder who can help us."

Ilyich remains for us the other, that one who deceived himself in ultimately self-destructive ways. For Tolstoy, if we are to avoid Ilyich's lot, we must first condemn and then transcend ourselves by taking a stand somewhere very distant from wherever we are now, or by managing somehow to make ourselves over as a child, or a peasant or a mystic. It may be that Percy's exercise also points ultimately toward the childlike and the mystical. But the path recommended to us by Walker Percy invites (or better incites) a playful acceptance of the self as it is now, not as we think it ought to be. It is an oddly graced and appealing approach, one that recognizes that the seeds of transformation are already present in the available self here and now, if only we look a little closer.

THREE LIES: A STUDY IN SPIRITUAL INDIRECTION

Philosopher Charles Taylor contends, in *Sources of the Self,* that Western civilization's ability to maintain its commitment to two essential elements of its cultural inheritance, self-affirmation and benevolence, has in recent centuries become more and more problematic. We just don't know how to care for ourselves and others at the same time.[14]

Taylor's observation suggests both a deep structural tendency within our culture to perceive benevolence and self-affirmation as mutually exclusive and an equally deep need to somehow resolve this tension. We cannot quite bring ourselves to explicitly renounce benevolence in favor of self-affirmation. Nonetheless, we may tacitly do just that. Our Ilyich-style reshaping of vocational discernment and moral sensibility to the contours of our self-seeking—material, social, and spiritual—represents our de facto surrender to an ethos of self-affirmation.

How can we be made aware of cultural and social forces that so powerfully and unobtrusively influence not only our thinking but also our life decisions? Reading social criticism and philosophy of culture can be helpful, but only marginally so. It's not that we don't get the gist of the arguments; it's just that they seldom hit home. Social and cultural presuppositions need to be encountered biographically, that is, in everyday conversation, as the backdrop against which decisions are made. The formulations of philosophy and social science, even when accurately depicting widely shared social and cultural assumptions, necessarily abstract themselves from the particularities of individual existence.

Given this, let me suggest that we alert ourselves to certain patterns of thinking that may encourage us to accommodate our moral and spiritual sensibility to the logic of scripted achievement. One simple activity that has proved helpful in ferreting out such patterns begins with imagining how we might respond to a certain request. For example, list and examine the thoughts and feelings, both positive and negative, that might arise if you were to be asked by a friend if you could volunteer, say, at a homeless shelter for two hours a week. After a short interval, examine only negative thoughts and reactions to this imagined request. I've noticed that, when I do this in class, since the expectation is that everyone is listing negative reactions, the awkwardness of moral competition is eliminated.

Over the years, I have made a point of collecting these negative reactions and grouping them into a dozen or so categories. Let me describe three such patterns of feeling and reasoning. The first I call "all or nothingness"; the second, "hopelessness of the cause"; and the third, "self-serving procrastination." Each pattern exemplifies a strategy by which a troublesome impulse toward compassion is remolded to allow free pursuit of socially scripted success. The point here, of course, is to invite you to uncover similar patterns of accommodation in your own life.

All or nothingness sounds something like this:

> If I were going to get involved in helping the homeless—and I can see that there is a great need for this—then I would give it my all. I wouldn't just work in a food bank or an overnight shelter for an hour or two a week. I would move to New York, give up my plans, my personal ambitions, and dedicate my life to helping the homeless. If I worked in a food bank for an hour or two a week, I'd feel like a hypocrite. I'd probably be doing it just to make myself feel good.

Not bad. Here, we are enabled to define ourselves as so sensitive that *were* we to do something to help the homeless we would give up everything to do so. Even better, by doing absolutely nothing, we can enjoy an invidious comparison with those who in fact volunteer each week for subtly selfish reasons. Note, additionally, the implicit acceptance of the cultural tendency to perceive benevolence and self-affirmation as mutually exclusive possibilities: either I go to New York and give up my plans, or I stay where I am and pursue them. Note, finally, how the self perceived as moral is tacitly assimilated into the projects and ambitions of the self envisioned as successful ("If I'm not going to New York and giving up my plans, then what the hell, I might as well see them through").

The all-or-nothing response is among the most commonly deployed, second only to the hopelessness of the cause: "The homeless problem is out of control. It's really sad. When I see those people, my heart goes out. But there's really nothing we can do about it. The politicians aren't really interested in solving the problem anyway. I have my own problems and responsibilities, and even though I may sound insensitive to some of you, I think I just need to stand back and embrace responsibility for my own life."

This variety of response is, perhaps, a little more convincing. But it rests on a kind of misplaced abstraction. Our friend did not demand that we solve the problem of homelessness but only asked that we consider volunteering at the shelter for a couple of hours a week. The implication again is that we feel strongly drawn to help. The desire to see ourselves as moral, as sensitive and concerned, is protected and maintained. In fact, the problem may be that we are a little too sensitive for our own good and that only our superior powers of analysis hold us back from giving our all. There is, once again, an implied invidious comparison between us and those well-meaning but naïve volunteers down at the shelter whose judgment is understandably clouded by sentimentality. The radical disjunction between benevolence and self-affirmation is once more evident: given the hopelessness of the cause, I might as well repair to my old haunts and get about the business of business, or the business of law or medicine or scholarship or pork belly futures.

One of my former students came up with the best example of self-serving procrastination I have heard. Though Ken's plan was offered tongue-in-cheek, it highlights by way of ironic exaggeration an extremely common pattern of response:

> Seeing the problem of homelessness makes me want to do something. I have a dream, and I'd like to share it with you. After I get a 3.9 GPA here at Colorado, I go to Stanford or Harvard or someplace that has a joint J.D./M.B.A. program. I graduate with honors, see, and then I go out and make a lot of money—four or five million anyway. Then, after a while, I get myself elected to the U.S. Senate. Once I'm there—and this is the beautiful part—I go on a hunger strike on the Senate floor until those clowns do something for the homeless.

Ken's plan hardly requires additional commentary from me. Its ability to sponsor a life of socially scripted ambition while receiving full moral credit is without parallel.

PRACTICES: MIRRORING AMBITION

Shortly after entering the Trappist monastery at Gethsemane, Thomas Merton had a laugh at his own expense. One evening on his way back from the sanctuary, Merton caught himself looking at his own reflection, hoping to find there the face of a monk. First, there was a moment of guilt, then the laughter set in. Merton had playfully uncovered an element of his envisioned self. Here was something to work with, something to ponder and pray about, something he might mention to his spiritual director. I think Dogen would have been pleased with his brother monk.

Dogen's point about studying the self to forget the self is a superb one. In this practice, our limitations, our ambitions, our inordinate attachments to multiple envisioned selves defined by our material, social, and spiritual self-seeking become something we never expected them to be. The very dross, the flotsam and jetsam of our interiority, that which our culture would have us repress, deny, or rationalize into respectability—all these become the very stuff of the self's transformation. *All* our ambitions, with *all* their constitutive illusions, distortions, and hopeless double kaleidoscopic improbabilities, no longer stand opposed to a life lived more fully in vocation.

As the gross metals of the alchemist are transmuted into gold, as the illusions and projections of romantic love find their unexpected fulfillment in mature commitment, so may ambition itself be transmuted into a life more fully given over to compassionate self-forgetfulness and quiet attentiveness to the longings of the heart. Ambition is the raw material of vocation.

Practice One: Family Resemblance

Reread the Percy exercise, this time attending less to its specific content and more to the feel of it.

What is it about Percy that invites us to explore the hidden fountains and gardens of our own interiority? How is it that he even gets us to peek at our sometimes murderous wish-images, the ones that echo Merton's pained confession that "I have what you have not. I am what you are not. I have taken what you have failed to take. . . . Therefore you suffer and I am happy, you are despised and I am praised, you die and I live; you are nothing and I am something"?

Consider this: "One morning . . . Suzuki Roshi gave a brief impromptu talk in which he said, 'Each of you is perfect the way you are . . . and you can use a little improvement.' "[15]

Is there a family resemblance between Walker Percy and Suzuki Roshi? Where is it most pronounced?

Practice Two: A Subtle Shift

Reflect on this sentence: "Ambition is the raw material of vocation."

Until this chapter, our focus has been on the felt opposition between ambition and vocation, between self-seeking and self-forgetfulness, between the envisioned self and the available self, whatever self is available to us in the moment. The felt tension is real because it is experienced as real. There is, however, no necessary or permanent disjunction, either experientially or theoretically. In fact, as the practice of spiritual indirection becomes habitual, the former felt antagonism between ambition and vocation and the rest undergoes a subtle shift.

Consider this passage from Dorotheos of Gaza (an Egyptian monk of the sixth century): "When passionate thoughts arise in the soul therefore, they are brought to light; this means that the workers of iniquity, viz. the inordinate passions, appear, in order that they can be completely destroyed for ever and ever."[16] How does Dorotheos' statement reinforce the felt tension between ambition and vocation, when ambition is taken as one

instance of inordinate passion? In what way does Dorotheos' statement confirm, on the other hand, the notion
that "ambition is the raw material of vocation"?

Remember Buechner's words about vocation? "The
place God calls you to is the place where your deep gladness and the world's deep hunger meet." Consider the
words that precede that sentence: "There are all different kinds of voices calling you to all different kinds of
work, and the problem is to find out which is the voice
of God *rather than* of Society, say, or the Superego, or Self-
Interest"[17] (italics mine).

Note, first, how Buechner's words faithfully describe the felt tension between ambition and vocation.
Now, rewrite his sentence so that it suggests a complementarity between ambition and vocation, that is, between God's call and all the other voices calling you.

Place the two statements side by side. Can you affirm both at the same time? At different times?

Practice Three: The Gift of Frustrated Desire

Trappist monk Thomas Keating has noted that "as we
begin the difficult work of confronting our own unconscious motivations, our emotions can be our best al-
lies. The emotions faithfully respond to what our value
system is—not what we would like it to be. . . . Hence
they are the key to finding out what our emotional pro-

grams for happiness really are." Keating continues: "We can learn to recognize our emotional programs for happiness by the afflictive emotions they set off. Basically, these emotions might be reduced to anger, grief, fear, pride, greed, envy, lust, and apathy" that emerge when "events . . . frustrate these desires."[18]

Let me suggest that the signifying character of the afflictive emotions may less often be traceable to frustrated covert desire alone than to a sudden or gradual realization of conflict between espoused values and covert desires. When the negotiated peace among the various strands of conscious and tacit self-seeking has been breached, we enter a moment of extreme vulnerability and unparalleled opportunity.

(1) Recall this passage from chapter three: "What is most telling about Ilyich's panting after social approbation is how quickly he jettisons his former moral code. Ilyich had always regarded his own heavy drinking and occasional philandering as vile behavior. But when he saw 'people of high standing' doing such things, though he did not immediately dismiss his own misgivings he felt considerably less perturbed. Soon he was not bothered at all."

(2) Reflect on how Ilyich was able to redefine his espoused moral sensibilities in a way that rendered them compatible with his social self-seeking.

(3) Consider the gradual shift from "being perturbed" to feeling "considerably less perturbed" to being "not bothered at all." Imaginatively reconstruct the modifications in Ilyich's internal conversation as he moved from the initial afflictive emotion of being perturbed to complete comfort with his once vile behaviors.

(4) How might Ilyich have explained away the significance of his afflictive emotions? Choose one:

- Residual guilt from his repressive Russian Orthodox upbringing
- It's only natural
- An innocent indulgence before marriage ("I'll get over it once I've settled down")
- Other (please specify)

Practice Four: Discomfort as Insight

Review the conclusion of the previous chapter, "Practice: Rationalization: A User's Guide," in which you traced back and studied your own rationalizations and avoidance techniques. Next, study the rationalizations and see if you can evoke the afflictive emotions to which they applied. What emotions did you feel? How did you explain away their significance?

Can you recall certain afflictive emotions, such as anger, jealousy, or frustration, that your rationalizations were intended to repress or redefine?

In the long run, did these afflictive emotions diminish or intensify? Were they instrumental in your finally confronting your own self-deception?

CHAPTER FIVE

Forgetting Ourselves
on Purpose

INSIGHT FROM SRI LANKA

Marilyn had recently returned from a stint in Sri Lanka
working with the Peace Brigades. The animating assumption behind the Peace Brigades is that the death
squads sanctioned by dictatorial governments in "Third
World" nations are less likely to murder or abduct someone accompanied by a citizen of the United States, Can-
ada, Germany, or some other "First World" nation. Of
course, that assumption is an iffy one at best, and volunteers know full well that they're standing in harm's way.

When Marilyn came to talk to our class, she told us
that upon arriving in Sri Lanka she took up residence
with a woman targeted for death by her own government. As far as Marilyn could tell, this woman faced im-

minent death for two reasons. She had witnessed the kid-
napping of her son—later found murdered—and she had
informed authorities that she could identify one of the
abductors.

During her stay in Sri Lanka, Marilyn experienced
what might be called a prolonged epiphany of recruitment. She told us that while she was in the company of
this woman, her life took on a kind of single-mindedness,
a directedness, that she had never experienced before.
There was no better place to be, nothing better she could
conceive herself doing, nothing else calling to her from
the wings, competing for her attention or evaluating her
performance. Her life was of a piece. She was alive—fully,
exuberantly, and incontestably. It's not that things were
pleasant, of course. Far from it. Marilyn spoke of the discomfort and disorientation she felt at having to move
from place to place to avoid her new friend's tormentors. There were other hardships, and there was danger
too, always threatening to take some tangible form.

The students were moved by her words. Not only
that, but for a number of students her story provoked
memories of their own, memories of similar recruitments of self-forgetful engagement or wounded empathy. Some seemed a little caught off guard by the
emotional force with which these memories emerged

into their consciousness and curious as to why they had forgotten them in the first place.

Of course, other guest speakers had awakened elements of the dormant shadow governments of compassion and idealism. That was the idea, after all. First, I would stir up their emotions by exposing them to suffering in one form or another. Then I would follow that up with inspiring depictions of saintly exemplars who knew just what to do in such circumstances. If these experiences proved powerful enough and the follow-up conversations cogent and encouraging enough, I thought someone might aspire to emulate these saintly types, if only part-time. Even though I would not have described my teaching this way at the time, and I certainly did not intend to manipulate my students' emotions, this "inspiration-aspiration" strategy characterized my teaching for several years. I had no idea what else to do. It seemed to me then—and I have seen nothing since to change my opinion—that the "inspiration-aspiration" approach is all but ubiquitous in the literature addressing issues of vocational discernment and spiritual transformation.

Nonetheless, well before Marilyn's visit, I had begun to sense the inadequacy of this approach. I had come to see that momentary recoveries of former epiphanies of recruitment evoked by exposure to the suffering of others quickly gave way to business as usual. They just didn't take. The initial aspiration response provoked by moments of intense inspiration, though often energetic, tended to fade quickly. In darker moments, I sometimes thought I could calculate the severity of the students' "compassion backlash."[1] There seemed to be a more or less direct correlation between the intensity of their initial emotional response and the speed and efficiency with which it would later be jettisoned.

They were on to me, some of them anyway, and they were pushing back: "What are we supposed to do once we've been touched by the suffering of others and have watched an exemplar or two march across our screens? What do you want from us, anyway?" Such questions, as far as I can tell, are neither flippant nor rhetorical. They are often asked with innocence and curiosity; they are sometimes voiced in a discouraged, even despairing, tone. But in one guise or another, the questions always arise.

Every so often, a particularly sensitive student challenges the inspiration-aspiration strategy with disarming emotional power. I remember one such instance particularly well. I was teaching my first class at Candler School of Theology, and we'd just finished listening to a deeply moving and beautifully crafted sermon about one man's embrace of a life of service in response to his father's deathbed request.[2] When, several minutes later, the tape suddenly snapped off, we were still sitting in silence. After a while, one, then two, now three students began to share their halting responses. I had trouble hearing one young man. His eyes were still red, and he was speaking very softly. I asked him if he could repeat what he'd said. "Sure," he said. "I felt set up."

Over time, I have learned that it's good to ask students directly about such things, about how they feel about being emotionally moved by depictions of human life *in extremis* by a teacher, inspirational writer, or another intent on sensitizing them to what they might otherwise have evaded. If you ask them, they'll tell you. But if these students were to speak with a single voice, I think they'd have something else to tell us "inspirational" teachers, something we'd rather not hear: "I've been touched before, recruited before, and I didn't know what to do about it then and I don't know what to do about it now. It just never seems to work out the way it should. All the things that have held me back before remain in place, and so do I. So what do I do about that?"

You can move people if you wish. You can reawaken a long-forgotten epiphany of recruitment if you think it's a good idea. You can lure a banished shadow government of compassion and idealism out of exile, if you have a mind to. But you can only do so a certain number of times before people catch on. No one likes a setup.

Surprisingly, the compassion-backlash formula did not prove out in Marilyn's case. Her words, her story, and the feelings and thoughts that were evoked from us that day were not so easily forgotten.

But why was her case different? Why was our response to her unlike our response to other guest speakers or inspirational readings? Her visit somehow embodied something other than the usual inspiration-aspiration approach.

Here was a vocational call enfleshed and unmistakable, self-validating in its immediacy and nearly overwhelming in its intensity. But it was not only or even mainly the certainty of her call, or the compelling character of her prolonged epiphany of recruitment, that she got across to us. That was part of it, of course. We believed Marilyn. And it didn't hurt that she was a poet and that her words cut close to the bone and moved the heart. But there was something else, something more important than what she had to say or how she said it. That something else was Marilyn's confusion.

Now that she was back in the States, back in Boulder, back teaching at the University of Colorado, she told us she didn't know how to answer the invitation she had received. She was frustrated and perhaps a little angry too. She felt pulled in a number of directions now. Little wonder: she had responsibilities to family, work, writing, and teaching. And even if she had the time, she wasn't sure how to make a connection like the one she had in Sri Lanka or how she'd be received if she tried. Things were just different here in so many ways.

Marilyn thought her confusion made her a pretty poor example. She thought maybe she'd set things in the class back a little. She was wrong. We believed her. We believed in the certainty of her call and her willingness to respond to it. But we loved her because she told us that she was confused and because she was worried about misguiding us. Not only that, but she presented us with a new possibility, one we had not really considered before. Despite all appearances to the contrary and the general drift of what we'd heard about the usual suspects, Marilyn's presentation implied something truly unexpected: you were allowed to speak about a powerful moment of recruitment with passion and in detail even though you really had no idea what to do about it at the moment.

This was a breakthrough. There were tears and laughter and shared stories after Marilyn spoke. As it turned out, many of us considered ourselves both recruited and confused and said so. It was in the class following Marilyn's visit that Martha told us about her "no big deal" recruitment at the orphanage. Other students began to recall similar moments of recruitment. One after the other, they prefaced what they said with a variation of the "no big deal" disclaimer, as is so often the case with a remembered epiphany of recruitment.

One of the students who had attended a prestigious prep school was ice-skating with a small boy from the inner city. It was nothing special, just one of those do-gooder things that do-gooder schools do, she said. She was putting in her time for a worthy cause. But the boy loved the skating and the music and said, "I'm going to dig a big hole and make me one just like this one when I get home." The memory of the quiet sense of wounded-ness evoked in her by these words had stayed with her for years.

Another student spoke of her summer as a camp counselor and of a camper who just would not let go of her the last day. It was funny at first, but then she sensed the desperation, the terror, of the camper who could not let go. She did not know what she was sup-posed to do. The image stayed with her, but now she thought it wasn't just about that child.

A young man spoke about his visit to a nursing home, about the fear that preceded the visit, about the sur-prising sense, once he was there for a little while, that he belonged, that there was no better place to be, and no better thing to do than to listen to an old man tell his stories. He didn't want to leave.

Yes, I know, we all cry at the movies, too. It doesn't mean much. We watch the nightly news and maybe we shed a tear for the children of famine or for refugees living in squalor. We may even feel a little better for having done so. But an epiphany of recruitment is not like that. It is not predictable. We cannot be manipulated into it by a screenwriter or newscaster, or by a professor; nor, surprisingly, is it easily correlated with the degree of suffering witnessed. We don't have an epiphany when we think we should. It's just not like that. There is mystery here.

Some experiences come to stand for others—who knows why. They emblazon themselves on our consciousness. They wound us and claim us. We are never quite the same, for despite all our attempts to marginalize or redefine them, we find that it is we who have been redefined.

We all knew what we were talking about that day. We were speaking about special memories, memories of great power, dangerous memories that we seldom recall, rarely speak about, memories tied intimately to our shadow government of compassion and love, memories discouraged and obscured somehow by other dreams and images we speak about with greater frequency and facility.

An epiphany of recruitment is not an end in itself; it is an invitation to a different kind of life. It's no use trying to extend the moment, or to recreate it. Nor need we flatten it out into some banal and sanitized image of moral or spiritual self-seeking. But neither can we expect to respond fully, immediately, and consistently to such a moment of recruitment. That was Marilyn's gift to us. She remembered her call, and she would not give up on it. She would talk about it, write about it, do whatever she could about it and await further instructions.

Her visit slowed us down too. Everything seemed just a little less urgent somehow. Why fall for the all-or-nothing take on things? What else is it that we thought we could do, anyway? Chasing our more compassionate envisioned selves into an idealized future is exhausting and dispiriting. Why not stay here and work with whatever we have available to us right now?

We got to wondering that day about how radically our lives might be transformed if, for a single month—no, for a single week, or even for a single day—we were able to simply notice and respond to the "no big deal" recruitments that met us from moment to moment. Our sense was that we'd probably end up in Sri Lanka, or its metaphorical equivalent, though we weren't sure what we meant by that or why we thought it.

Marilyn's visit reminded me of a story, one I failed to tell the class. The man on the bus was on his way to a job interview. He was traveling to Boulder from Denver and told me and the driver that he needed to get off somewhere on Broadway. He seemed a little disoriented and kept repeating for all to hear that it looked as if he would finally get a new job. Soon, he singled out a few of us to share the good news in greater detail. He was celebrating, with the innocence of a child. It looked for all the world as though he finally had what he wanted, and he needed to talk about it.

Today was the big interview at something-something Broadway, and he was dressed to the nines. He showed me the letter he had been waving around when he got on the bus. My heart sank. The Broadway he wanted was back in Denver; he was already in Boulder, more than twenty miles from where he needed to be.

The driver shook his head and gave him a pass to go back. I got off the bus with him at a shopping center about a mile from downtown Boulder, and we talked until his bus came. While we were waiting, he told me that he didn't like his old job because his friends made fun of him. They said he was stupid. He asked me why they said that. I told him I didn't know. The people at the new job were nicer, he told me. "I talked to that one guy on the phone. He was really nice."

"That's good," I said. "Maybe things will be better now."

I watched his bus disappear down Broadway heading for Denver. It was cold, but I walked home anyway.

THEY'RE NOT HYPOCRITES; THEY JUST FORGOT

The Youth Theology Institute (YTI) is a month-long intensive summer program held here at Emory's Candler School of Theology. YTI gathers highly gifted young people, rising high school seniors, from across the country, who share an interest in theology. These "scholars"— that's what we call them—study together and get involved in service projects and, more important, exhaust one another in late-night conversations about the mysteries of God, faith, and sexuality. As I write this, I'm in the midst of teaching a highly condensed version of my Ethics of Ambition course for YTI. We meet at my apartment now, a short walk from campus, since the classroom we were assigned in Woodruff Library had a tundralike climate and a landscape to match.

A couple of days ago, I got a call from Latta Thomas, a counselor at YTI, inviting me to join his service team for a trip to Montgomery, Alabama. Latta told me that his team was going to visit Bryan Stevenson, a young African American graduate of Harvard Law School who heads up a team of lawyers working with death row inmates in the Alabama state penitentiary. Tim Van Meter, another counselor, had mentioned to Latta that I had assigned an article about Bryan to my Ethics of Ambition class.[3]

The article, which had appeared in the *Washington Post Sunday Magazine* a number of years ago, leans ever so slightly to the hagiographic side. Nonetheless, it never fails to elicit strong response and to surface all kinds of things that might otherwise remain unsaid. The author, Walt Harrington, is fascinated and confused by Bryan. "Simply put," Harrington says, "the man is hard to figure." Even his parents were confused by his decision to work with death row prisoners and wondered out loud why, after working so hard at Harvard, he wouldn't, well, just take the money.

Speaking with Bryan's friends only intensified Harrington's confusion and fascination. One friend told him "that you will not find anyone who doesn't say that Bryan is a saint." The *saint* label, or some variation on it, such as "prince of a man," or "angel," is pretty much run of the mill when it comes to describing Bryan. Taking momentary leave of his own agnosticism, Harrington wonders out loud if Bryan might not be one of the thirty-six *lamed-vovniks*, the anonymous righteous ones of Jewish legend "sent by God to live and work among us."

As you might expect, Bryan is less than amused by this consensus beatification. The words they speak about him, he says, are really not about him at all; they are about their own longings, about their own desire to live a different kind of life: "When people say I'm great, what I'm doing is great, they aren't talking about me. They're talking about themselves, about what's missing in their lives."

I think Bryan has a point. When we read the Harrington article, especially those parts when he's talking with Bryan's friends, our admiration for Bryan is tinged with an edge of sadness. Like Marilyn, Bryan is not as easy to dismiss as the usual suspects, who can, with little effort, be reduced to ascetic icons intoning a solemn invitation to a life of self-abnegation and repressed desire. Bryan likes to play around a little. He turns the questions back on you, puts the shoe on the other foot.

Maybe Bryan really is a *lamedvovnik*, who knows. But for me he resembles nothing so much as a walking invitation to a life lived more fully in vocation. He is good at shaking up the habitual patterns of response and tired presuppositions we use to hide things from ourselves. When asked directly why, after all, he did not take the money, he expressed dissatisfaction with the question: "What people don't understand when they say I could be making all this money is that I couldn't be making all this money. . . . If the death penalty were abolished tomorrow, I wouldn't be a corporate lawyer; I'd probably be a musician."

Upon our arrival at the Gallagher House in Montgomery, the service team was ushered into a small law library. We filled the dozen or so chairs arranged around the meeting table. Bryan arrived on the scene within a couple of minutes. He began by telling us about his work and a little about his life as well. After twenty minutes of speaking, he concluded by telling us how the deck was stacked against the young black men in America both on and off death row.

A couple of the scholars were not overly sympathetic. They were not unmoved by what Bryan said, but they wondered about the victims and their families; they wondered if the men Bryan defended didn't really have themselves to blame.

Bryan heard the scholars' concerns and addressed them in measured tones. He told us that his own grandfather had been brutally murdered, stabbed to death, stabbed dozens of times. That crime and crimes like it were, yes, unspeakable, evil, incomprehensible. He would make no excuses. Speaking of the perpetrators of such crimes, he said he simply didn't believe in "killing them back." But Bryan was insistent that the justice system was not color-blind and repeated with quiet passion his concerns about young black males coming of age in America.

Then he told us a story.

At the time, Bryan was living in Atlanta, not all that far from where the scholars were housed at Emory. One night, he was making his way back to his apartment in his ancient and battered Honda Civic, when something marvelous and unexpected occurred. Every once in a while, Bryan explained, his otherwise useless radio would, in response to a bump in the road, suddenly spring to life. Bryan savored such moments. Well, his car must have hit a bump just right this time, because the radio played on and on, and Bryan sang his heart out as he drove through that hot Atlanta night.

But things got even better: a Sly and the Family Stone three-hit marathon came on, and Bryan was really into it. As he pulled up at his apartment complex, he just had to extend the magic for another moment. "Everyday People," his favorite from Sly's repertoire, had just come on, and he wanted to sing it through.

Suddenly, everything changed. He looked out the window of his Civic and watched as a police car pulled up beside him. Another squad car appeared. One of the officers emerged from the car with his revolver pulled. Bryan slowly stepped out of the car and stood up facing the officer. Rattled, the policeman aimed his revolver at Bryan's head. Frozen where he stood, Bryan did not dare to draw a breath, convinced that if he moved he'd be shot dead. He heard the officer speak, and he put his hands over his head and then leaned up against his old Civic. As the officer and his partner questioned him, a crowd gathered. As the last chords of "Everyday People" played out, Bryan heard his neighbors talking: "Maybe he's the one who broke in and took my fan." "Yeah, I think I've seen him hanging around here before." "There are things you don't hear about that happen around here all the time."

For days, Bryan was haunted by thoughts of what might have happened to him. What if he'd moved, what if he'd resisted? He flinched when he thought about it. He couldn't sleep. The scene played over and over again in his mind. "If I'd been a younger man, I *would* have moved, I *would* have said something, and I *would* have died."

It was a week or two later, after his fear had abated somewhat, that different but equally chilling thoughts came to plague Bryan. "What about my nephews; what about my cousins; what about other kids who would not have known what to do, who would have acted out of fear, anger, and confusion?" Bryan was "deeply burdened" by these thoughts. They would not let go of him. He had to do something about it.

On the way to Montgomery, I had shown Ethel Johnson a copy of the Harrington article. Ethel was YTI's seventy-something Wise Person in Residence—a title that seriously underestimated her capacities. Long-time civil rights activist, friend and compatriot of Malcolm X, and retired seminary teacher, Ethel was the spiritual glue that held our summer academy together. She told me that I should get Bryan to sign the article on the back. Then I could copy it and bring it back to the Ethics of Ambition class.

"C'mon, Ethel," I said, "that's really cheesy." Ethel stared at me with a mixture of amusement and befuddlement that I'd seen before.

"Brian," she said firmly, "just do it. I'm sure the students will appreciate it."

So toward the end of our time with Bryan, I overcame my lingering sense of cheesiness and asked Bryan for his autograph. "I was wondering, Bryan, if you could write a little message to the students from my class who weren't able to be here today. You could write it here on the back page of this article. I'll get it copied. I'm sure the students will appreciate it."

"By the way," I found myself saying, "I worry a little about some of my students, some of the students here, for instance, who are so idealistic when they are young and seem to forget about it all when they get a little older. I don't know if you remember, but Harrington reported in that article about you that 70 percent of your entering classmates at Harvard said they planned to practice public-interest law and that only about 3 percent ended up actually doing so. What do you make of that, and what can be done about it?"

Bryan was holding the pen just a little above the article I'd handed him. "You know, I don't think they were hypocrites," he answered. "They meant what they said. I really think they did. When they wrote their statements for the admissions people, they were telling the truth. But it's hard to remember what you really want when you're being pursued by big law firms a little later and everybody's talking about it. People change in law school. They forget what brought them there."

He put the pen down. "My suggestion is pretty simple, if you're looking for a suggestion. I think it would be a good thing if those students just carried that application statement around with them and read it once in a while. It would make a difference, I think. It would help them remember why they wanted to go to law school in the first place. It's not about giving things up, it's about what you really want."

He wrote for a few seconds and handed the article back to me:

To the Ethics of Ambition Class:
Keep your eyes on the prize. Hold on.
—Bryan Stevenson

WOUNDED AUDACITY

When I got home from class the day Marilyn visited, the first words I wrote in my diary were "Blessed woundedness." Then I wrote it again, more forcefully this time: "Blessed woundedness." Why these words? I'm not sure. Those were the words that came to me. I didn't choose them.

I wondered: Doesn't St. John of the Cross speak about a "blessed wound" somewhere in *The Dark Night of the Soul?* Is that it? No, that isn't quite it.[4] The words, the sentiments came from somewhere else. The echoes were more distant than that, and a little more intimate too. "We can rest in this blessed woundedness as we can rest nowhere else," I wrote. "There is no better place to be." Then it came to me: those two prayers I said every night when I was a kid. I tried to recite them. But I was conflating the two, leaving things out and getting frustrated with myself.

The next day, I walked over to church and filched a hymnal from the pew after discovering that the prayers were printed on the inside of the back cover. The *Anima Christi* contains this special petition: "Within your wounds hide me; separated from you, let me never be; from the evil one protect me; at the hour of my death, call me; and close to you bid me; that with your saints, I may be, praising you forever and ever."

The Prayer Before a Crucifix expresses a strong desire to live a different kind of life as a response to Jesus' own loving woundedness: "O kind and gentle Jesus, I kneel before you and pray that you would impress on my heart the virtues of faith, hope and charity, with true repentance for my sins and a firm purpose of amendment. At the same time, with sorrow I meditate on your five precious wounds, having in mind the words which David spoke in prophecy. 'They have pierced my hands and my feet, They have numbered all my bones.'"

I know there's a problem with this kind of language. Speaking of "blessed wounds" to those already wounded is problematic. But blessed woundedness is not about attraction to sickness and pain; it is not about self-hatred or the diminution of selfhood or the exploitation of women or minorities.

It's hard enough to point to a shift from self-scrutiny to self-forgetfulness as a deep source of joy. But why the imagery of woundedness? Why so gloomy? What about softer tones and a gentler touch? Blessed woundedness, though, is not something added or recommended. It is something called forth, evoked.

Time and again, year after year, maybe once or twice during our time together, sometimes more often, a silence descends on the class when we remember how we have been wounded by the pain of others, and how profoundly and desperately we have wished to respond with our whole heart, soul, and mind. We speak softly of our failures to respond adequately and how these failures confuse and sadden us. But the spirit of such silence does not allow guilt. There is peace instead. It is as if, in admitting what we have tried to hide from ourselves, we no longer need to fear sudden exposure of our inauthenticity. More than once when this spirit is upon us, someone will say something like "Let's give it all up and live in a commune together somewhere out in the mountains." Sometimes I feel the same way. It's just too hard to remember what's important on your own.

But maybe the language of blessed woundedness is not as troubling as I think. There are others who use similar language to express the deepest longings of the heart. Denise Levertov speaks of the "audacity" and beauty of Julian of Norwich's powerful desire for the paradoxical beatitude of blessed woundedness:

Swept beyond event, one longing
outstripped all others: that reality,
supreme reality,
be witnessed. To desire wounds—
three, no less, no more—
is audacity, not, five centuries early, neurosis;
it's the desire to enact metaphor, for flesh to
    make known
to intellect (as uttered song

makes known to voice,
   as image to eye)
make known in bone and breath
(and not die) God's agony.[5]

Jean Vanier is the founder of L'Arche, which describes itself as a network of communities of people with developmental disabilities and those who share life with them. Vanier speaks of "a wound of peace in which Jesus lives." "Through this wound," he says, "I can approach others without barriers, without the fears and aggression I often feel, . . . without the waves of egoism."[6] And Henri Nouwen speaks of the messiah, who, according to a legend in the Talmud, is sitting among the poor, covered with wounds, rebinding his wounds one at a time rather than all at once, so that he will be ready when he is needed.[7]

BEATITUDE: FEELING THE PLEASURE OF GOD

Bryan Stevenson's parents played a video for Walt Harrington. It was a tape of Bryan preaching to the national youth conference of the African Methodist Episcopal Church. They told Harrington that after they'd watched the video, they finally understood what their son was doing with his life and why Bryan couldn't just take the money. "I didn't understand his faith until this talk," his father said. "He never talked about himself ever."

"We've got to be prepared to pay the cost of what it means to save our souls," Bryan told the young men and women at the youth conference. Then he read from Matthew 25: "'Oh blessed of my Father, inherit the kingdom prepared for you from the foundation of the world, for I was hungry and you gave me food; I was thirsty and you gave me drink; I was a stranger and you welcomed me; I was naked and you clothed me; I was sick and you visited me; I was in prison and you came to me. . . .'"

"I wouldn't exchange what I'm doing for anything," Bryan said, voice rising. "I feel the pleasure of God."

"God's pleasure," "God's agony." Who knows how to talk about it? If our wounded response to the wounds of others points the way to beatitude, if these audacious longings are truly not neurosis five centuries later, then there is really no way to say so politely, no way to please our therapists, our professors, and our bowling team.

Two years after Marilyn's visit to class, I was browsing through the periodicals at Woodruff Library here at Emory, when I came across a poem she had written for the *Kenyon Review*. The poem told of things she had not mentioned to us. Reading it, I could see now that she'd gone easy on us. Still, it was the same story. She'd managed to get it all across somehow. I wondered to myself,

Is this poem Marilyn's memory of wounded recruitment? Does she recite it every so often? Does it help her remember what she once knew and knows again in reciting these words?

I was in my fields when I heard the first shots
I walked quickly   The houses were empty
I could hear the soldiers ahead, firing
Then I met others, also walking quickly

We came to Kumaranayagam's mill
Beside the gate red blossoms of hibiscus
The gate stood open   Beyond I saw my wife
She stood in the compound as though she
  owned nothing

Inside a strip of light lay across the floor
A woman knelt dipping a cloth in a bucket
Again and again she washed the same stain
The stain began to gleam, as though polished

My wife had laid our children side by side
She had placed the smallest between the
  other two
She had laid the boy between his two sisters
They liked to walk that way, one on either
  side[8]

Sometimes I think our dangerous memories of wounded recruitment are made remote by design, are purposely exiled to the far reaches of consciousness to languish in the shadowy company of other dissident beliefs, dreams, hopes, and one-time fevered intentions. They don't fit with what we've come to expect will really make us happy; that is to say, they do not jibe with the ascendant scripts of success and distinction characteristic of our time and place. We are well tutored in the ways of reductionism and irony. We're just not going to be set up again if we can help it.

When you come right down to it, our epiphanies of recruitment and our memories of them are like beatitudes. Beatitudes, if nothing else, are dependably disruptive of whatever it was that we thought we really wanted. Blessed are those who mourn and weep? Blessed are the poor in spirit? But formative remembering doesn't just happen; it is an act of will, awakened and guided by grace. Formative remembering does not rehash and celebrate a one-dimensional depiction of some envisioned self to be pursued, even if the image claims to portray the self as self-forgetful. Formative remembering points to our intentional, ritualized, and repeated attempts to dwell within what we have encountered both in our epiphanies of recruitment and the wisdom of our sacred traditions.

Together, formative remembering and the practices of spiritual indirection present an alternative to our culture's reflexive advice regarding the good life: envision and pursue. The alternative is this: remember and resist.

PRACTICE: DAYS OF REMEMBRANCE

OK, get up, grab a pen, and find your calendar. Now, block out four days, not more than three months down the line, but no less than a week or two from now. Write the words "days of remembrance" in the space you have reserved. Write over something if necessary.

In the time leading up to your days of remembrance, reflect on the meaning of epiphanies of recruitment and ponder what events in your life qualify as such. Remember that epiphanies of recruitment are often dangerous memories, almost inevitably at odds with the ascendant social scripts of our culture. For that reason, they are often repressed and unavailable to immediate recall. Try not to confuse such symbolic moments with the "big deal" experiences often associated with maudlin sentimentality, with the kind of emotional manipulation found in Christmas specials or greeting cards.

As you prepare for your days of remembrance, it may prove helpful to divide your "life tapestry" into decades, or even smaller segments, spending several hours reflecting on each, over a period of several days.[9]

With the help of a spiritual director or a group of like-minded companions, plan out a retreat schedule for your time away. Include sufficient time for rest, for extended periods of silence, for liturgy, for study of sacred texts, and for conversation with a trusted adviser (or group).

Spend several hours each day reflecting on how you have responded to an epiphany of recruitment you have identified. Grieve and celebrate the response.

On the final day of your retreat, address yourself in detail to these two questions proposed by Thomas Merton: "If you want to identify me, ask me not where I live, or what I like to eat, or how I comb my hair, but ask me what I think I am living for, in detail, and ask me what I think is keeping me from living fully for the thing I want to live for."[10] Respond from the depths of your heart.

Be patient with yourself. If, during your retreat, you experience resistance, especially if resistance takes on the character of guilt or shame, remember the bad Buddhist horse and its odd and paradoxical advantage. Or reflect for a moment on these words I heard Archbishop Tutu address to the fine Christian horses at Emory's Candler School of Theology: "You know what your problem is? I will tell you what it is. You just don't have any idea how low God's standards are. They are very low . . . very, very low, indeed. Remember, you cannot do anything to make God love you more, and you cannot do anything to make God love you less."

REMEDIAL PRACTICE

If you feel that you don't have the time for a four-day retreat, you may wish to consider this alternative: a five- or six-day retreat.

If you balk at spending so much time away from your responsibilities but claim that "I'd just love to go if I weren't (1) working with the indigent (or with my patients, or my clients, or [fill in the blank]); (2) doing the Lord's work in the world (or Muhammad's or Shakyamuni's or Coca-Cola's); (3) supporting a family with two kids in college and a huge mortgage hanging over my head; or (4) the sole caretaker for my aging parents," then please try this exercise on for size.

Write an imaginary but candid dialogue between yourself and whoever it is you're caring for that's preventing you from making this retreat. Sample dialogue fragment: "I think it might be valuable to go on this five-day retreat. Who knows, it could even be a life-transforming experience for me. But I'm not going to go because of my commitment to your welfare." Reflect on how these words might be received by your "dependent" conversation partner. Then respond in writing as you think your interlocutor might respond.

If you're speaking with a child under age ten, imagine a conversation some twenty years from now, in which you explain to the adult sitting across from you with a gin and tonic in hand why you didn't make the retreat. Be sure to share your musings about how it might have made a difference in your life, if only you'd been free to go.

CHAPTER SIX

The Meritocracy Machine

HARVARD AND OTHER PROBLEMS
WITH ADMISSIONS

A couple of years ago, I ran across an article in the *New York Times Magazine*. I'm always on the lookout for new material, but it's rare to come across something so perfect that I find myself at the copy machine with no recollection of having left my chair. The article in question, "Inside the Meritocracy Machine,"[1] provides a vicarious sense of what it must feel like to be a gifted and ambitious high school senior waiting to hear if Harvard wants you for next year's freshman class.

The stakes are high and the odds steep, and the four seniors profiled in the article know it. Harvard, "the nation's most prestigious university," the author tells us, is able to accept only a relatively small proportion of the twenty-nine hundred valedictorians (let alone all the other applicants) who apply for two thousand freshman slots. The dean of admissions at Harvard, trying hard not to sound triumphal, says that Harvard could reject all its first choices and select an equally exceptional second class from its applicant pool.

On April 4, the day before the students, from Van Nuys, California, were to hear from Harvard, the four of them huddled outside school, "trying to talk themselves out of wanting it so much." One student, who had scored a perfect 800 on her SAT in math and had already been accepted by Berkeley, was now having second thoughts about going so far away from home. Was Harvard really worth it? Another spoke of the admissions process being "brutal" and "random" and told the others about her sister's bad experience with Harvard a few years back. A third student, who, though Polish by extraction, could speak and read Mandarin Chinese, offered that if she attended Harvard, it would only be "for its reputation." The fourth student, Maya Turre, a young woman who ranked tenth in her class but was also principal violinist in the community orchestra and undefeated in twenty-nine varsity tennis matches, said that she probably wouldn't go to Harvard because Harvard didn't offer a major in architecture. Harvard, she said, ranked fourth on her list at the moment.

As things worked out Maya was the only one accepted. Immediately after receiving word of her acceptance, she admitted to feeling confused. Reached by phone a short time later, she told the *Times* journalist, "Well, I'm leaning toward Harvard."

The four Van Nuys students who were profiled remind me of the young men and women whom I taught for three summers at the Youth Theology Institute. Both groups have evolved intriguing strategies of self-protection to armor themselves against the emotional consequences of falling short of their expectations. The rising seniors at YTI, like their counterparts in Van Nuys, sometimes need to talk themselves out of wanting admission to a particular college too badly. But there is a difference between the YTI students and the students described in the *Times* article. Students at YTI often (though not always) employ religious language, the language of the Christian narrative—its sacred stories, historical traditions, and espoused values—to hide from themselves and others the power that some of their hidden desires exercise over their lives.

Like the rest of us, these young men and women are deeply, energetically, and anxiously invested in the images of success propagated by the meritocracy machine and, like many of the rest of us too, are just a little uncomfortable with the fact. The anxiety that accrues from living with this inevitable ambiguity over time tempts them, as it tempts us, to enlist elements of the Christian narrative to smooth the agitation through gentle acts of redefinition—that is, by convincing themselves that as true Christians, they don't worry excessively over college admissions and things like that. We cannot live without consolation, after all, and where else can we turn if not to the resources of our faith? Whether fully conscious of the fact or not, we often seek out the psychological equivalent of "plausible deniability" around the emotionally charged issues of success and failure.

Of course, the more strident our claims that the Christian narrative affords us a uniquely reliable critical perspective over and against social norms, the more plausible and effective our strategy becomes for masking our investment in those same norms. In effect, we often claim to have already transcended these norms before we admit or even realize how significant they are for our lives. Ironically, many of the most influential among contemporary Christian educators and their theological mentors aid and abet us in our subterfuge by stressing time and again, and with little sensitivity to either personal idiosyncrasy or social context, the radical over-and-againstness of our shared faith story vis-à-vis the stories of our culture.

Although I admit the limitations of my own educational context and personal vision, I wish to state strongly and unambiguously as a religious educator that the last thing the young men and women I teach at YTI need—young men and women who, after all, give up a month of their summer vacation to attend a Christian theological institute—is additional encouragement in claiming that their Christian faith has already triumphed over their secular ambitions. Such uncritical affirmation of the efficacy of selected Christian beliefs and practices allows easy detachment of personal faith from personal ambition, effectively giving the latter free reign and reducing the former to a consolation prize for those who fall short in the arena of cultural competition. By placing a premium on denying the power that secular success stories already exercise over their imagination, we inadvertently encourage these young men and women to keep up appearances—Christian appearances—at all costs.

Such an attempt to tame and regulate the volatile relations between the Christian story and cultural script by claiming that faith simply trumps secular ambition can be misleading. If I say that because of my faith, being rejected by Harvard didn't really bother me, I may well be telling the truth; but it is not inconceivable that I am using my faith as a strategy for rationalization. And that would be a shame. The consolation of faith cuts so much deeper than that, allowing as it does for real failure and renewed hope.

The internal conversation between the narratives of faith and culture is to one degree or another already falsified, both collectively and individually. We are, many of us, already adept at distorting the Christian narrative either to legitimate our dubious successes or to deny actual failures. For this reason, a critical task of Christian practice is not so much to correct the very real distortions of the cultural story with the pure witness of the Christian story as it is to unmask, repent, and then refashion the particulars of the inevitable distortions between faith and culture already in place. Here again, I am speaking of the practices of formative remembering and spiritual indirection. It is essential to ask ourselves and each other, and our churches too, what it is we are living for and what is it we think is keeping us from living fully for the thing we want to live for.

We do not transcend our ambitions so much by claiming to have already risen above them as by slowly, patiently, and faithfully working our way through them, at ground level and in the company of friends. Otherwise, we too eventually come to suspect what many non-Christians already suspect: that we are simply fooling ourselves.

The inadequacy of the uncritical over-and-against strategy of Christian formation to effectively resist the allure of worldly success is exemplified in a theological reflection on the life of Nazi war criminal and former chief architect for the Third Reich, Albert Speer, written by Stanley Hauerwas and David Burrell.[2] Speer's situation parallels those of Ivan Ilyich and John Dean in that he, as they, appears unable to hear the bells ring, unable to respond to the tocsin call that warns of imminent moral collapse. Speer, again like Ilyich and Dean, is culpably inattentive to his own experience at least in part because of the power of his professional ambitions. As Hauerwas and Burrell observe, Hitler had offered Speer "what every professional dreams of, the opportunity to make his wildest ambitions come true." He was not about to give it all up. When a friend of Speer's warned him never to visit Auschwitz, Speer decided he would not ask him why. From that moment on, Speer writes, "I was inescapably contaminated morally; from fear of discovering something which might have made me turn my course."

How can we account for Speer's refusal to see where his ambitions were leading him? Hauerwas and Burrell think the reason Speer did not finally address his own self-deception was that he embraced a story "inadequate to articulate the engagements he would be called upon to undertake." For Hauerwas and Burrell, it is the Christian narrative that presents a story adequate to the task of ongoing self-discovery and conversion: "The saints formed by this story testify to its efficacy in purging the self of all deception as it forces the acceptance of a new self mirrored in the cross." It is the narrative itself, according to the authors, that forces us to face our deceptions and purge ourselves of them.

Who knows? It may well be that Speer could have been delivered from his moral contamination by recourse to the Christian narrative and the communal support and liturgical practices that accompany it. But this might-be deliverance is far from certain. Had Speer been formed by the Christian narrative, he would nonetheless have been tempted to either compartmentalize or distort his appropriation of Christian faith to accommodate an overwhelming passion for success. In this he would not have been alone. Himmler, perhaps the second most powerful figure in the Third Reich and a regular at Sunday services, had himself reached such a demonic accommodation, as had many other Christians in the Nazi Party.

Despite the power and forcefulness of their message, Hauerwas and Burrell leave us exactly where we started. It was the students' (and our) use of the Christian narrative to obscure a deep investment in the symbols and reward systems of the meritocracy machine that initiated these considerations in the first place.

But what alternatives can we recommend? It is here that the practice of indirection—that is, uncovering and gently resisting what we think is keeping us from living fully for the thing we want to live for—comes into play again. Recall Walker Percy's self-help quiz from Chapter Four. It was not until we admitted that we did not feel empathy for Charlie that we were able to unmask and perhaps playfully repent our jealousy over his socially scripted success story and his new yacht.

Falsifying the internal dialogue between Christian faith and cultural script can take many forms. One strategy of falsification unwittingly adopted by many of us is born of the need to live up to the norms and visions of Christian faith. We are admonished to watch ourselves and others closely to make sure that we're doing it right, that we're living in congruence with the demands of the Christian story. We have our programs and our score cards and our red pencils at the ready.

But it was William James, that notorious tutor of liberal religious educators, who first called our attention to the fact that self-centered enjoyment of observing our successes in this world is not limited to material and social self-seeking but also includes the nobler egoism of spiritual self-seeking.[3] It is not easy to admit that Christian formation inevitably appeals to such self-seeking even as it moves to undermine and transform it. Thomas Merton may have been thinking something of the sort when he offered that Adam and Eve probably wished to learn the difference between good and evil not so much because they planned on choosing evil, but because they wanted to watch themselves being good.

PRACTICE: REASONS AND RATIONALIZATIONS FOR THE ADMISSIONS COMMITTEE

Please write an essay addressed to us—the admissions committee of Harvard College—explaining why you'd like to attend Harvard; why you wouldn't like to attend but probably will anyway if admitted; why you probably will attend but really shouldn't; or why you probably should attend, if admitted, but will most likely fail to complete this application out of fear of rejection.

In addition, please inform us—the admissions committee of Harvard College—which rationalizations for feigning indifference concerning your admission to Harvard you find most convincing. (Have you fully exploited the resources of your religious tradition to provide high motives and plausible narratives to aid you in this endeavor?)

The admissions committee would also like to know whether your favored rationalizations concerning why you care so little about being admitted to Harvard College might, ironically, obscure the fact that you truly do not wish to attend Harvard.

Please tell us as well what image you have of your-self as a Harvard graduate some four or five years from now. (Feel free to draw in the space provided on the re-verse side of application, beneath the watermark.) What kinds of feeling do you associate with being a Harvard graduate? Do you expect that people might treat you dif-ferently once you have graduated? What specific images of your graduated self do you most enjoy entertaining in the drawing rooms of your imagination?

Finally, if you have not already addressed this ques-tion in your application essay, please do so: Are you always, usually, or only occasionally able to distinguish rationalizations from reasons in your analysis? Do the two thought processes feel different from one another? If so, how?

Nota bene: If you are a legacy, please bypass the essay question and print clearly, in the space provided below, the name(s) of family member(s) who have attended Harvard College or Radcliffe College. Print first name first, last name last, and middle initial in the middle.

HARVARD DIVINITY SCHOOL AND OTHER PROBLEMS WITH ACCEPTANCE

The high school students from Van Nuys had their own reasons for telling themselves that they did not want to be accepted at Harvard. As an Irish-Catholic townie already at Harvard Divinity School, I told myself I didn't want to be accepted either. I had my reasons too. The Van Nuys students associated Harvard with academic excellence, with prestige, with success, with the American dream. And so did I. But I also associated Harvard with a particular cadence and accent that were not my own. There are words I associate with Harvard too—dignified words, authoritative words. But some of these words brought pain:

> My grandfather thought for a moment, as if what he was going to say surprised him. "Well," he said, "to tell the truth, I rather wanted to vote for Kennedy. . . . He seemed an extremely attractive fellow." I could fill in the pause at the end of the last sentence: "for an Irish Catholic." Like most Bostonians of his class and time—any time since the 1840s, actually—my grandfather loathed the Irish. The children of any other ethnic group—Jewish, Italian, German, blacks (though I don't think he knew any blacks)—my grandfather was more than happy to consider for friendship or potential friendship. . . . But not the Irish.[4]

The words are from *Old Money* by Nelson Aldrich, and the sentiments they express, I suspect, lingered longer in Cambridge, Massachusetts, than anywhere else (save Northern Ireland). I felt words of this kind in my bones and in my heart, and like my friends and family I took an unspoken oath never to admit that they hurt.

For that reason, I had to find a way to be "at" Harvard Divinity School without being "of" it. I liked the courses; I wanted the degree. All in all, it was the kind of place I'd hoped it would be. Still, I could not afford to see myself through "their" eyes. To do so would, as I saw it, be to disparage myself and my family and to be disloyal to my anonymous relatives who fled the Potato Famine to arrive in Cambridge—yes, in the 1840s and, yes, just in time to hear Mr. Aldrich's words, or something just like them.

In nineteenth-century Ireland, the Catholics who took food from Protestant missionaries were called "soupers." The message: Don't take the soup; it is better to starve than to convert. My strategy was a little different, and somewhat less extreme. I figured that if I could make myself into nothing in much the same way that mystics do, then I would never fall to the temptation to think I was really something because I was part of the Harvard crowd.

Sitting for prolonged periods of silence in a pew about halfway back in the sanctuary of St. Paul Church, just outside Harvard Square, I enlisted Thomas Merton as my guide as I set out on the path of self-negation. St. Paul's was my sanctuary. My father had gone to grade school there and had sung in the choir. Tom Gately, my great-uncle, was the sexton there decades before I arrived on the scene, and I'd attended Mass there off and on since high school.

Merton proved a good companion, and I usually carried a copy of New Seeds of Contemplation to church with me. I underlined sentences and phrases first in one color and then in another. I scribbled irretrievable notes in the semidarkness of late afternoons. So often did I dog-ear pages that when New Seeds was lying on its side it appeared half again its normal size.

Merton's words demanded and provoked careful self-examination. He was not like the theologians I was reading at Harvard Divinity School, even the ones I liked best. With Merton, it wasn't a matter of simply getting the point, of following his argument. Perhaps I learned best from Merton when I put the book down, pausing to wonder, to savor, to pray. I was especially attentive to anything Merton wrote about the gift of nothingness: "And the most precious of all the gifts of nature or grace is the desire to be hidden and to vanish from the sight of men [sic] and be accounted as nothing by the world and to disappear from one's own self-conscious consideration and vanish into nothingness in the immense poverty that is the adoration of God."[5]

Becoming nothing, however, proved more difficult than I had imagined. First of all, it was unclear just what nothingness was and how to take aim at it. I considered several possibilities. Maybe desiring to be nothing meant that I stopped trying to be somebody in the sense of the phrase "He really thinks he's somebody." Or, accepting the gift of nothingness could mean loving God and others so perfectly that I'd become nothing to myself as a kind of inevitable by-product. Then again, Merton said being nothing was a gift. Do you ask for the gift of nothingness by name? What did God want me to do?

As I initiated what I judged to be appropriate realignments of my personhood toward increasing nothingness, I found Merton's descriptions of the true self–false self dichotomy most helpful, diagnostically speaking. The true self was in fact something very much like my desired state of "nothingness in God." Ambition, ego, self-seeking, avarice, lust, Harvard, trying to be somebody—all these were the provenance of the false self. Clearly, if I could root them out, I'd be moving toward nothingness at a pretty good clip. Merton warns: "Our external, superficial self is not eternal, not spiritual. Far from it. This self is doomed to disappear as completely as smoke from a chimney. It is utterly frail and evanescent. Contemplation is precisely the awareness that this 'I' is really 'not I' and the awakening of the unknown 'I' that is beyond observation and reflection and is incapable of commenting upon itself."[6]

Wanting to be "of Harvard" was to invest in the smoke and mirrors of the false self. Common Harvard descriptors, such as "the Yard" and "the College," assured me beyond a doubt that this was an institution passionately and irreversibly committed to its own something-ness. There would, of course, be moments of temptation, moments when I might secretly desire to become a man of substance, by sharing in Harvard's mystique. I toyed with the idea of buying a Harvard sweatshirt once. Luckily, Buddy Linehan's dad was the cop on duty that day at the Harvard Coop, and I walked away uncompromised ("How's it goin', Mr. Linehan?").

Harvard might have *the* Yard and *the* College, but my mentor, Thomas Merton, had apparently retained significant elements of his own nothingness within the incomparably substantial somethingness of the Roman Catholic Church, "the only *The* Church," as the eminent American historian Martin Marty once called it. In fact, Merton had already proved his value in this sacred arena by helping me remember that faithfulness to God was not identical with maintaining some impossible standard of moral purity, nor was it a matter of trying to live up to someone else's vision of sainthood: "For me to be a saint means to be myself. Therefore the problem of sanctity and salvation is in fact the problem of finding out who I am and of discovering my true self."[7]

But sometimes Merton confused and angered me. He seemed to take away with one hand what he'd just given with the other. He never seemed to pass up an opportunity to inform me that the very practices he'd recommended a moment ago were themselves prob-lematic. Worse yet, Merton sometimes made it sound as though trying to be nothing might just be a way of trying to become something, still another subtle man-ifestation of the dreaded false self: "Even when I try to please God, I tend to please my own ambition, His enemy. There can be imperfection even in the ardent love of great perfection, even in the desire of virtue, of sanctity. Even the desire of contemplation can be impure, when we forget that true contemplation means the complete destruction of all selfishness—the most pure poverty and cleanness of heart."[8]

Rightly or wrongly, I sometimes thought that what Merton was asking of me was to cultivate a kind of blank self, a self in name only, a self that allowed things to push it around without ever pushing back, a self that had no right to the space it took up or to the air it breathed, a self that, far from being self-forgetful in God, was incessantly vigilant, always watching itself, for fear that at any moment it might again tumble back into the smoky evanescence of the false self.

I was relieved years later to discover that others who had learned from Merton and still held him in the high-est regard had harbored similar doubts. Distressed by Merton's notion of "the annihilation of the self" and his description of someone who has achieved this exalted spiritual state as one "who is dead and buried . . . and . . . no longer exists among the living who crawl about in time," Ann E. Carr wonders about Merton's own self-hatred and the popularity of a book recommending a "vision of self-annihilation in God."[9]

But Merton seems to have his own doubts about the same matter. Toward the conclusion of *New Seeds of Contemplation*, he offers what seems like a contemplative's equivalent of an apology and retraction, one that takes a new and more graceful tack regarding the false or exterior self. Merton says: "Appearances are to be accepted for what they are. The accidents of a poor and transient existence have, nevertheless, an ineffable value. They can be transparent media in which we apprehend the presence of God in the world. It is possible to speak of the exterior self as a mask: to do so is not necessarily to reprove it. The mask that each . . . wears may well be a disguise not only for [the] inner self but for God, wandering as a pilgrim and exile in His own creation."[10]

Merton's description of the redeemed external self is highly sacramental in character. The external self as the "transparent [medium] in which we apprehend the presence of God in the world" evokes an image of the gifts of bread and wine brought to the altar before communion. The bread and wine, we know full well, still embody our ambitions and all our shortcomings, as well as our true longing to praise, to worship, to serve, to love. Then God transforms them, and we are in turn transformed.

During this period of intense preoccupation about my nothingness before God, I often attended daily mass at St. Paul's. I would like to think that I could sense, even if I could not yet name, my own need and desire to "offer up" my intense spiritual self-seeking to God as a gift during the offertory. Did it occur to me at the time that I could just relax, let myself off the hook, and simply leave my feverish attempts to amount to nothing at the altar? Did I sense that God would gladly receive whatever I had available to give at the moment? Perhaps I did. After all, I had precedent for this kind of thing. When, as a little kid, I would present still another dandelion bouquet to my mother, fresh from our backyard, she would time and again express her delight at such a wonderful gift from her son. Maybe God accepted my ambitions for nothingness with even greater delight. Whether I actually thought and felt this way as I approached communion, I am not really sure.

One thing I do remember is that when I left my pew and walked up to the communion rail at St. Paul's, William Alfred was usually somewhere ahead of me in line. Professor Alfred routinely sat two or three rows in front of me and a little to the right, his crumpled fedora beside him. I knew little about him except that he taught English at Harvard and that he had written a play and donated the proceeds to build a new roof for the church.

About two years ago, I read that William Alfred had died. Piecing together things from the Web, I learned more about his life. Born in Brooklyn in 1922, Alfred was the son of a bricklayer and a telephone operator. His lyrical play, *Hogan's Goat*, about turn-of-the-century Brooklyn-Irish politics, had a long and successful off-Broadway run. Counted among his friends were Seamus Heaney, Robert Lowell, Elizabeth Bishop, Bill Murray, Gertrude Stein, and Faye Dunaway. But Alfred was also considered an easy touch. "He probably befriended more undergraduates than any teacher in the school's history," said one friend. It was also common knowledge among the poor and working-class residents of his neighborhood that you could always count on William Alfred for a couple of bucks. A Harvard colleague, arriving at Alfred's small home as an unexpected visitor late one evening, was surprised when Alfred answered the door with money in hand. The Rev. Peter Gomes, Harvard's Professor of Christian Morals, called him "our Celtic saint."

But the sentence that really caught my eye was this one: "William Alfred was one of the great unknown men of this century."[11] I hadn't known that about him. I'd never spoken to him, except when we exchanged the sign of peace before communion. It sounds like he could have helped me out with my nothingness problem. He must have been really something.

PRACTICE: ALTERNATIVE READING SKILLS

- Reread this passage from Thomas Merton: "And the most precious of all the gifts of nature or grace is the desire to be hidden and to vanish from the sight of men [sic] and be accounted as nothing by the world and to disappear from one's own self-conscious consideration and vanish into nothingness in the immense poverty that is the adoration of God."[12]

- In his book *Compassion and Self-Hate*, Theodore Isaac Rubin relates an anecdote about spiritual pride. He describes a rabbi and a cantor, both prostrate before the Holy Book on the Day of Atonement, Yom Kippur. The two are outdoing each other proclaiming their unworthiness before the Lord of the Universe. "I am nobody, nothing. . . ." "I am nobody and nothing at all. . . ." "I am dust." Meanwhile, Moishe the janitor enters the temple and, hearing the cantor and the rabbi, begins to follow suit. As Rubin tells it: "In a tiny, reedy voice he also implores God to regard him as 'a nobody, a piece of dirt, nothing at all, absolutely a nobody and nothing. . . .'

Then the Cantor notices, listens to the janitor and with quiet derision pokes the Rabbi, points to the janitor and says, 'Look who thinks he's nothing.' "[13]

Can you read the Merton passage above as inciting this sort of spiritual pride? Can you find within yourself the capacity to look down on all those less evolved among your friends and acquaintances, who are still caught up in the pathetically banal search for wealth, fame, and power and who have not a hint about the profound spiritual wisdom of being accounted as nothing by the world?

■ James W. Fowler, in *Becoming Adult, Becoming Christian*, lists a series of consequences of understanding our lives in terms of vocation. Fowler's listing takes on the character of a beatitude. Consider his summary of what it means to be "in vocation":

> First, in vocation . . . we are called to realize excellence as a result of God's addressing us, but not with the motive of outstripping others. . . .
>
> Second, this understanding of vocation frees us from anxiety about whether someone else will fulfill our particular destiny before we get there. . . .
>
> Third, to be in vocation frees us to rejoice in the gifts and graces of others. In vocation, we are augmented by others' talents rather than being diminished or threatened by them. . . .
>
> Fourth, freed from jealousy and envy, able to celebrate the gifts of others, we are freed from the sense

of having to be all things to all people. . . . In vocation we can experience our *limits* as gracious, even as
we can experience our gifts as gracious.

Fifth, . . . vocation is the opposite of workahol-
ism. . . . [We are] freed from the need to ground or
vindicate our own worth. . . .

Sixth, in vocation . . . we are freed from the
tyranny of time. . . . Vocation . . . says that we are
called into time; we are given life. In fidelity we understand that we are also given death, whenever it
comes.[14]

See if you can read Merton's passage as inviting you
to embrace a life more fully in vocation, a life free from
jealousy and envy, a life less driven by the need to vindicate your own self-worth, a life in which you can actually experience your limits, perhaps even your faults,
as gracious.

- You have just concluded a conversation with your
supervisor, who'd "love to keep you on board but didn't
want you to overlook the advantages of early retirement."
As you stare in stunned silence at the shiny green folder
containing all you'll need to make your decision, you turn
to the passage from Merton for comfort.

Can you read Merton's words as giving you a credible rationalization of your own failure or expectation

of failure? After all, what your supervisor thinks about you amounts to next to nothing. And your job, well, that was just your job, not your vocation.

- Rather than judging any of these three readings as simply correct or incorrect, consider that all three may pertain to how you actually receive Merton's invitation at a given moment. Consider further that this is perfectly all right, and in fact could hardly be otherwise.

Now, imagine approaching the altar with the bread and wine of the only self available to you at the moment— you know, that self with the complex mixture of pride, self-loathing, true longing, that self already incipiently in vocation and yet still substantially "in ambition." Consider this gift of the only self you have available to you at the moment to be just the gift God wishes to receive from you.

Picture yourself praying after you have received Holy Communion, asking God to empower you to remember what you are living for, and to see with clarity and without undue guilt and shame what is keeping you from living fully for the thing you want to live for. Pray also that you are allowed to realize that you are thus already fully in vocation and that there is no place else you need to be, nothing else you need to do. Feel free to dance quietly at your pew.

PRACTICE: PLANNING AN ALTERNATIVE
NEW YEAR'S CELEBRATION

What's wrong with New Year's resolutions? Why do they so seldom take hold, so frequently lead to discouragement, self-recrimination, or February's brooding fatalism? I would say that New Year's resolutions by and large suffer from the same error that characterizes many reform movements. Would-be reformers often indulge in the rhetoric of replacing—lock, stock, and barrel—something thought to be deeply distorted with something thought to be much better, something idealistic, something pure and brand spanking new. On the face of it, this seems like a pretty good idea.

Terry Eagleton has warned against the temptation to embrace the kind of "premature utopianism" that "grabs instantly for a future, projecting itself by an act of will or imagination beyond the compromised political structures of the present." His point is a good one and has immediate implications for the approaching New Year.

So if you'd like to bypass the tiresome and ineffectual routine of projecting and pursuing your vastly improved self for yet another year, you may wish to plan a simpler New Year's Eve. Consider an alternative celebration in which you simply promise yourself to attend to the "compromised structures" of self available to you in the present moment. Why go to all the trouble of adding something new? That's God's business, not yours, and it has already been taken care of. "Each moment," Merton counsels, "brings with it germs of spiritual vitality. . . . We must learn to realize that the love of God seeks us in every situation, and seeks our good."[15]

But I don't want to mislead you here. Your alternative New Year's Eve may prove somewhat less intoxicating than last year's. Let me present you with a gentle challenge. You may find it difficult to admit that you are more than a little addicted to the rush of replaying the images of your all-new, I-really-think-I-can-do-it-this-time self. I'm not asking you to go cold turkey. You won't need to pull the plug on them. Remember, your addictions are themselves part and parcel of the compromised structures you'll be nurturing. For now, I'd say, try not to encourage them. Leave them alone. And by all means invite them to your party. They'll be there anyway, and this way you'll get to keep an eye on them.

Here's another helpful question you'll want to consider: What is it exactly that your compromised structures have compromised? What once called you out of yourself but now only whispers? Which truths dream themselves powerfully at night but fade at daybreak? Which sufferings implored you to bind their wounds and to tell their stories?

Ask your epiphanies of recruitment and your shadow government of compassion and idealism where they've been keeping themselves, and tell them you're sorry if it was anything you said. They may be reticent. They have reason to be. Some have been exiled, others ridiculed. A few have received death threats. Call them. Maybe you could visit them at home. In fact, you might want to consider moving in with them and having your alternative celebration there. They're an odd bunch, but they say it was you who left home, and they'd really love to have you back.

Afterword: Occupations and Preoccupations

Vocation finally is less about discovering our occupation than about uncovering preoccupations. We can leave our work at the office, but our preoccupations ride home with us. They sleep with us too, and they dream with us. Our preoccupations are what loved ones sometimes tell us we care about more than we care about them.

But how do we know that our pursuit of the elusive different kind of life we call vocation isn't finally just more self-seeking, the pursuit of still another envisioned self, another . . . well, ambition? How are the preoccupations of vocation different from those of our ambitions and our envisioned self?

Tad Dunne, a retreat director trained in the tradition of Ignatian discernment, arrives at the conclusion that two things seem to catch Jesus' attention and to preoccupy him during his public ministry: pain and joy.

Jesus noticed pain wherever he walked and was sought out by those in pain. The very sign of the Kingdom of God is the healing of those who suffer. For Dunne, "noticing pain is a path to noticing love."[1] Attending to the suffering of others is not the work of self-seeking, even spiritual self-seeking. Nor is attending to suffering a matter of living up to the demands of an idealized compassionate self. Attending to suffering is simply seeing what we see when our eyes are not closed, averted, or glazed over. Attending to suffering is not about adding something to ourselves at all. Attending to suffering in the world is a gentle practice, not a harsh ideal, and just the kind of thing we do when we aren't so busy, so fearful, so preoccupied.

The joy that Jesus noticed is the joy evoked by the parables of the Kingdom of God. It is the joy imparted in the unsettling good news of the beatitudes: blessed are the discounted, the written off, the losers, the hopeless idealists. It is the joy of the prodigal son, and even more so of his father. It is the joy of the criminal crucified next to Jesus. Jesus' joy is, finally, "the joy of homecoming." Joy preoccupies God, and it preoccupies God's Son and God's Holy Spirit. We are invited to share in this joy.

But let me add quickly that the preoccupations of God and of Jesus and the preoccupations that construct our ambition games are not in stark opposition. This is not to say that we cannot be seduced away from what it is we truly want, or that we are not complicit in our own seduction. It is only to say that God can transform our silly games (and our society's) and make them into something entirely new. God can take advantage of the scripted falsifications of our culture even as they take advantage of us.

In Chapter Four, I employed the metaphor of transmutation, of alchemy, to describe a welcome complementarity between our ambition games and our deeper calling. I said that as the alchemist's gross metals can be transmuted into gold, so our ambitions can be transmuted into a life more fully given over to compassionate self-forgetfulness and quiet attentiveness to the longings of the heart. But all in all, there's more of transubstantiation than transmutation at work here. I believe that the bread and wine of all our daily activities—once we let go of them, once we offer them to God—can be transformed by God's love, the perfect love that casts out fear. No arcane knowledge can transmute our deceptions into truth, our games into service, our self-centeredness into love. This is the provenance of God alone.

Still, we can cooperate. We are children of God, of course, and like most children we are often preoccupied with our own games and with winning them. Nonetheless, we leave our games and head home every so often, just to make sure we're loved—loved whether we're winning or losing or just passing the time. Gerald May, of the Shalem Institute for Spiritual Formation, says that "the longer we live, the more we ache to be loved for who we are rather than what we do. This longing goes so deep that I have never met a person who could not be moved to tears at the full realization of it."[2]

Of course, in playing our games we are often cruel. We get into fights; we say things we'd like to take back. We get hurt, too. We forget that all of our playmates are from the same neighborhood. Worse than this, evil can pervert and distort our games, as jealousy and rage cloud our minds and misguide our will. We protect our winnings with violence and embrace the ways of hatred. We have murder in our hearts. But God sends emissaries and prophets and His own Son to call these things to our attention, to suggest that we grieve and repent them and start anew.

There are implications here for the invitation to the general dance, the invitation that Thomas Merton passed along from God. The dance is for children, and as such it is hardly choreographed at all. It is a spinning and giggling dance, a crying dance. It is a bump-into-each-other-and-fall-down-and-get-up dance, a dance in which we sprint impulsively in one direction and then another. It is a skipping, hopping, scraping-your-knee kind of dance. It is the dance of pain and it is the dance of joy.

PRACTICE: CAPTAIN MIDNIGHT AND OTHER
FAILED PROJECTION DEVICES

One of the small disappointments of my childhood can be laid at the feet of Captain Midnight. In a memorable episode, Captain Midnight had once again vanquished disgruntled aliens trying to defend their home planet. Things got a little iffy for a while, however, and the Captain was forced to hide out in the mountains to avoid detection. At a crucial moment, Captain Midnight deployed an intriguing supra-high-tech device that projected his swaggering image onto a cloud bank, revealing his exact position to his comrades-in-arms.

When informed by an authoritative voice that this same high-tech imaging device was now available to the general public for a quarter and an Ovaltine label, I sensed that I needed to act quickly. Standing by the gate to my backyard, secure in the shadows cast by my three-decker, I stared up at the late-afternoon sky. There it was—my billowing face rising majestically above Chilton Street for all to behold. Could they see me from Harvard Square? Does the thing come with a microphone?

When Captain Midnight's high-tech device arrived in a decidedly small envelope, my heart sank. Who could forget the frogman disaster and how my brother, my sister, and I "trailed baking soda all over the damned house" in the vain hope that our plastic Lloyd Bridges would dive to the ocean's floor? Our baking soda–powered nuclear sub was an even bigger flop: it bobbed on its side instead of diving. Glancing at the size of the cardboard box that contained the projection device, I wondered how I'd allowed myself to hope again. Captain Midnight's high-tech projection mechanism was nothing more than a plastic-rimmed, thumbnail-sized mirror. I was so disheartened, I didn't even bother to try it out.

Perhaps our adult projections of our multifarious self-seekings are less brazen, less straightforwardly self-aggrandizing, than those of our childhood. I still try to project my image onto cloud banks, sometimes in hope of being rescued from the alien intruders of aging and death. It still doesn't work, but I'm having fun catching myself at it. I'm living in a new neighborhood these days. Sometimes—a little more often than in the past—I simply watch the clouds as they pass by. They never hold their shapes very long.

Where are you living these days? Do we need to catch up?

Notes

PREFACE

1. This definition from *Webster's Seventh New Collegiate Dictionary* is cited in J. Epstein, *Ambition: The Secret Passion* (Chicago: Dee, 1980).

2. For an account of the notion of self-appropriation, see the Introduction to B.J.F. Lonergan, *Insight: A Study of Human Understanding* (New York: HarperCollins, 1978).

3. W. James, *Psychology (Briefer Course)* (New York: Collier, 1962).

4. T. Merton, *New Seeds of Contemplation* (New York: New Directions, 1961), p. 297.

5. Sister Rose thinks I'm uncomfortable with my body because I'm Irish. I think she's wrong. Nonetheless, I am reminded of James Joyce's description of Mr. Duffy, who "lived at a little distance from his body." J. Joyce, "A Painful Case," in *Dubliners* (New York: Penguin, 1976), p. 108.

6. T. Merton, *My Argument with the Gestapo* (New York: Norton, 1975), pp. 160–161.

CHAPTER ONE

1. F. Buechner, *Wishful Thinking: A Theological ABC* (New York: HarperCollins, 1973), p. 95.

2. R. Coles, "A Boy's Journey from Liberalism to Social Darwinism," in *Children of Crisis*. Vol. 5: *Privileged Ones: The*

Well-Off and the Rich in America (New York: Little, Brown, 1977), pp. 269–289.

3. Coles, "A Boy's Journey," p. 274 (italics in original).

4. Coles, "A Boy's Journey," p. 288.

5. H. R. Niebuhr, *Faith on Earth* (New Haven, Conn.: Yale University Press, 1989), p. 100.

6. I do not mean to imply that epiphanies of recruitment are a function of the intensity of the feelings aroused in a given moment. Nor does the term *epiphany* suggest the unmediated experience of some reality that forces itself on us. I agree with Charles Taylor that the reality the epiphany embodies "is not the bare scene, but the scene transfigured by emotion. And the emotion, in turn, is not simply personal or subjective; it is a response to a pattern in things which rightly commands this feeling." C. Taylor, *Sources of the Self: The Making of the Modern Identity* (Cambridge, Mass.: Harvard University Press, 1989), p. 475.

7. D. Coupland, *Life After God* (New York: Pocket Books, 1995), p. 359. I would like to thank Beth Corrie for pointing out this passage to me.

8. R. Coles, *The Spiritual Life of Children* (Boston: Houghton Mifflin, 1990), pp. 326–327.

CHAPTER TWO

1. The several quoted passages are from H. L. Mencken, *The Vintage Mencken*, ed. A. Cooke (New York: Vintage, 1955).

2. R. M. Huber, *The American Idea of Success* (New York: McGraw-Hill, 1971), pp. 105–106.

3. P. L. Berger, *The Sacred Canopy: Elements of a Sociological Theory of Religion* (New York: Doubleday, 1967), pp. 23–24.

4. James, *Psychology*, p. 198.

5. James, *Psychology*, pp. 202–205.

6. *Invidious comparison* is a term first used by University of Chicago sociologist Thorstein Veblen to describe the process of "comparison of persons with a view to rating and grading them in respect of relative worth or value." The object of such comparisons, according to Veblen, is to allow those who make such comparisons to embrace "the relative degrees of complacency with which they may legitimately be contemplated by themselves and by others." T. Veblen, *The Theory of the Leisure Class* (New York: Viking, 1931).

7. James, *Psychology*, p. 201.

8. W. James, "The Will to Believe," in J. J. McDermott (ed.), *The Writings of William James: A Comprehensive Edition* (Chicago: University of Chicago Press, 1977), p. 727.

9. S. Weil, *Waiting for God*, trans. E. Craufurd (New York: HarperCollins, 1973), p. 210. I first came across this quote in R. Coles, *Simone Weil: A Modern Pilgrimage* (Woodstock, Vt.: Skylight Paths, 2001).

10. A. De Mello, *The Way to Love* (New York: Doubleday, 1991), pp. 1–3.

11. If, by the way, the thought just occurred to you that you probably need to reconstruct my strategy for reconstructing De Mello's practice, you are of course correct. You are also too smart for your own good and need to consider the inhibitive potential of your habitual embrace of suspicion. Sure, you can be duped into self-deception. You can also be duped into sidestepping essential insights owing to your inveterate tendency to remain in what amounts to a cognitive holding pattern. So you're fearful of ever touching ground; you'd rather circle than crash. I'm with you there all right. Then again, consider the fact that there's only so much fuel, so much energy for this kind of deal. You're going to have to resume your approach pattern soon enough or you'll crash anyway. Go ahead if you need to: reconstruct my reconstruction as you do all of your own, but try to remember, in the process of doing so, that your deconstructive proclivities are part

of the narrative also and are not without their own wiles and weaknesses. Write them down, draw them, ask somebody else you trust about them. Don't let your proclivities talk you out of it, either. Put them on an advisory committee, but don't let them run the show. Frankly, I'm not so sure they care whether you crash or not.

12. For an excellent treatment of the notion of "self-defining experiences" in relation to "unitive experiences," see G. G. May, *Will and Spirit* (San Francisco: HarperSanFrancisco, 1982), pp. 96–100.

CHAPTER THREE

1. L. Tolstoy, *The Death of Ivan Ilyich* (New York: Bantam Books, 1981), pp. 133–134. (Originally published 1886)

2. Tolstoy, *Death of Ivan Ilyich*, p. 53.

3. Tolstoy, *Death of Ivan Ilyich*, p. 66.

4. Tolstoy, *Death of Ivan Ilyich*, p. 52.

5. Tolstoy, *Death of Ivan Ilyich*, pp. 123–124.

6. Tolstoy, *Death of Ivan Ilyich*, pp. 126–127.

7. J. Dean, *Blind Ambition* (New York: Simon & Schuster, 1976). John Dean was implicated in the cover-up surrounding the June 17, 1972, break-in at Washington's Watergate residence and office complex that ultimately led to President Nixon's resignation. Dean was charged with obstruction of justice and served four months in prison. G. Gordon Liddy, a former FBI agent who helped plan the Watergate break-in, served four and a half years. He is currently a talk show host in the Washington, D.C., area. Howard Hunt, a former CIA agent, organized the bugging of the Democratic headquarters at the Watergate and served thirty-three months in prison. He is the author of several spy thrillers. John Ehrlichman served as assistant for domestic affairs in the Nixon White House. Ehrlichman was convicted of perjury and conspiracy to obstruct justice. He spent a year and a half in prison. (www.

washingtonpost.com/wp-srv/national/longterm/watergate/front.htm)

8. Dean, *Blind Ambition*, p. 31.

9. Tolstoy, *Death of Ivan Ilyich*, p. 120.

10. P. Chödrön, *The Wisdom of No Escape and the Path of Loving-Kindness* (Boston: Shambhala, 1991), p. 8.

11. S. Suzuki, *Zen Mind, Beginner's Mind* (New York: Weatherhill, 1988), p. 38.

12. Luke 15:7.

CHAPTER FOUR

1. Epstein, *Ambition*, p. 1.

2. Merton, *New Seeds of Contemplation*, p. 48.

3. We do not expressly hold such views, of course. This is to say, we would not affirm belief in such nonsense; we're more re-alistic than that. We know life is more complex and that happi-ness is not so easily attained. However, when we objectify our unconscious programs for happiness and examine the behaviors they incite, the logic of our pursuit will often approximate what in the light of day we would label as both foolish and naïve.

4. R. Nozick, *Philosophical Explanations* (Cambridge, Mass.: Harvard University Press, 1981), p. 597.

5. F. Nietzsche, *The Birth of Tragedy and the Genealogy of Morals*, trans. F. Golffing (New York: Doubleday, 1956), p. 299.

6. Exodus 20:19.

7. The term *programs for happiness* is borrowed from T. Keating, *Invitation to Love: The Way of Christian Contemplation* (Rockport, Mass.: Element, 1992).

8. Dean, *Blind Ambition*, p. 129.

9. B. W. Moore and G. Weesner (eds.), *Hidden Gardens of Beacon Hill* (Boston: Beacon Hill Garden Club, 1987), p. 38.

10. While visiting Ireland for the commemoration of the 150th anniversary of the Great Irish Famine, I visited the Famine Museum in County Roscommon. My father's forebears were from that county and immigrated to the United States during that period. The Famine Museum is located in the stables of one of the "big houses," the former property of the notorious absentee landlord mayor, Denis Mahon, who was assassinated in 1847. Many of Mahon's tenants were for all practical purposes coerced to emigrate. See S. J. Campbell, *The Great Irish Famine: Words and Images from the Famine Museum* (Strokestown Park, County Roscommon, Ireland: Famine Museum, 1994).

11. *The Friends of Eddie Coyle,* by George V. Higgins, is a well-crafted detective novel set in Boston. Spenser and Hawk are familiar characters in Robert B. Parker's detective novels. John Cuddy is Jeremiah Healy's creation.

12. W. Percy, *Lost in the Cosmos: The Last Self-Help Book* (New York: Farrar, Straus & Giroux, 1983).

13. Percy, *Lost in the Cosmos,* pp. 64–65.

14. C. Taylor, "Visions of the Post-Romantic Age," in *Sources of the Self: The Making of the Modern Identity* (Cambridge, Mass.: Harvard University Press, 1989).

15. " 'Stay Exactly Like That': Stories of Shunryu Suzuki Roshi Told by His Students," ed. D. Chadwick, *Shambhala Sun,* May 2001, p. 50.

16. *Dorotheos of Gaza: Discourses and Sayings,* trans. E. P. Wheeler (Kalamazoo, Mich.: Cistercian, 1977), p. 197.

17. Buechner, *Wishful Thinking,* p. 95.

18. Keating, *Invitation to Love,* pp. 19–20.

CHAPTER FIVE

1. I thank Elise Boulding for suggesting the term *compassion backlash.*

2. F. Craddock, "Cloud of Witnesses" (audiotape) in *Recorded Sermons of Fred Craddock* (Atlanta: Candler School of Theology, Emory University, n.d.).

3. I wish to thank Allison Pease for calling this article to my attention.

4. The words I had in mind may well have been these:

> All who are free
> Tell me a thousand graceful things of You;
> All wound me more
> And leave me dying
> Of, ah, I-don't-know-what behind their stammering.

St. John of the Cross, *A Spiritual Canticle of the Soul and the Bridegroom Christ*, trans. K. Kavanaugh, OCD, and O. Rodriguez, OCD (Washington, D.C.: ICS Publications, 1991).

5. D. Levertov, "The Showings of Julian of Norwich, 1342–1416," in *Breathing the Water* (New York: New Directions, 1987), p. 76.

6. J. Vanier, *Community and Growth: Our Pilgrimage Together* (Toronto: Griffin Press, 1979), p. 118. Thanks to Michael Hryniuk for pointing this passage out to me.

7. H. Nouwen, *The Wounded Healer* (New York: Doubleday, 1975).

8. M. Krysl, "Suite for Kokodicholai, Sri Lanka," in *Warscape with Lovers* (Cleveland, Ohio: Cleveland State University Poetry Center, 1997), p. 12.

9. I recommend the exercise "The Unfolding Tapestry of My Life" in the appendix of J. W. Fowler, *Faith Development and Pastoral Care* (Philadelphia: Fortress Press, 1987).

10. Merton, *My Argument with the Gestapo*, pp. 160–161.

CHAPTER SIX

1. B. Weber, "Inside the Meritocracy Machine," *New York Times Magazine*, Apr. 28, 1996.

2. S. Hauerwas with D. B. Burrell, "Self-Deception and Autobiography: Reflections on Speer's *Inside the Third Reich*," in S. Hauerwas with R. Bondi and D. B. Burrell, *Truthfulness and Tragedy: Further Investigations in Christian Ethics* (Notre Dame, Ind.: University of Notre Dame Press, 1977).

3. See James, *Psychology*.

4. N. W. Aldrich Jr., *Old Money* (New York: Knopf, 1988), pp. 89–90.

5. Merton, *New Seeds of Contemplation*, p. 174.

6. Merton, *New Seeds of Contemplation*, p. 7.

7. Merton, *New Seeds of Contemplation*, p. 31.

8. Merton, *New Seeds of Contemplation*, p. 43.

9. A. E. Carr, *A Search for Wisdom and Spirit: Thomas Merton's Theology of the Self* (Notre Dame, Ind.: University of Notre Dame Press, 1988), p. 26.

10. Merton, *New Seeds of Contemplation*, pp. 295–296.

11. From the Web site of the radio program *Connection*, produced by WBUR in Boston. (http://www.theconnection.org)

12. Merton, *New Seeds of Contemplation*, p. 174.

13. T. I. Rubin, *Compassion and Self-Hate* (New York: Simon & Schuster, 1975), pp. 70–71.

14. J. W. Fowler, *Becoming Adult, Becoming Christian: Adult Development and Christian Faith* (San Francisco: Jossey-Bass, 2000), pp. 83–85.

15. Merton, *New Seeds of Contemplation*, pp. 14–15.

AFTERWORD

1. T. Dunne, *Spiritual Mentoring* (San Francisco: HarperSanFrancisco, 1991), p. 93.

2. May, *Will and Spirit*, p. 73.

The Author

Brian J. Mahan, a Catholic layperson, teaches at Candler School of Theology, Emory University.

Index

Spiritual success, failure in, story of, 51–55
Sri Lanka, experience in, 126–127
Standards, 154, 171
Stein, G., 175
Stevenson, B., 138–142, 143–144, 148–149
Subpersonalities, 36
Success: constricting images of, 30; expectations for, 6; failure in, stories involving, 38–45, 51–55, 66–77; images of, investment in, 158–159; perceived, 39–40; self-evaluation of, 61, 62, 65; types of, 42, 43, 44, 62, 64
Suffering. See Pain and suffering
Sullivan, J. L., 105
Summer camp scenario, 133
Superego, voice of, 122
Suspicion, 4–5, 6, 7, 29, 43, 44, 62; adherents of, 8; discouraged by, 13–14; habitual, 191n11; origin of, looking for, 15; of over-and-againstness, 161–162; questioning, 91; respite from, 64
Suzuki, S., 83, 120–121
Sympathetic people, 48, 49

T
Talmud legend, 148
Taylor, C., 114, 190n6
Thomas, L., 137–138
Tocsin, 74, 162
Tolstoy, L., 66, 67, 69, 70, 71, 72, 74, 75, 99, 100, 101, 111, 112, 113
Transcendence, 161
Transformation, 113, 119–120, 135–136, 174, 185
Transmutation, 120, 185

Transubstantiation, 185
True contemplation, 172
True self, discovering, and sainthood, 171
True self–false self dichotomy, 170
True success, 42, 43, 44, 62, 64
Turre, M., 157–158
Tutu, D., 153–154

U
Ubiquitous lie, 72–73
Universal cooperation and congruency, 94–95
Universalizing, 99, 100
University of Chicago, 28
University of Colorado, Boulder, 1, 29
Unscripted life, 10–11, 32; longing for, 41

V
Valentino, R., 38–42, 43, 45, 48
Value system and emotions, 122–123
Van Meter, T., 138
Vanier, J., 148
Veblen, T., 191n6
Vocation: characteristics of, 183; defining, 10–11, 13, 44; living fully in, example of, 138–144; possibility of, 113; raw material of, 120, 121, 122; traditional connotation of, 9; understanding, consequences of, 177–178
Vocational call, experiencing. See Epiphanies of recruitment
Vocational discernment, 91, 114; model of, 45–46
Volunteering, request for, responses to, 115–119
Vulnerability, 44, 123